Southern Living®
ANNUALS & PERENNIALS

Oxmoor House®

Southern Living
ANNUALS & PERENNIALS

Library of Congress Catalog Number: 98-67026
Hardcover ISBN: 0-8487-1837-2
Softcover ISBN: 0-8487-1854-2
Manufactured in the United States of America
First Printing 1998

Editor-in-Chief: Nancy Fitzpatrick Wyatt
Editorial Director, Special Interest Publications:
Ann H. Harvey
Senior Editor, Editorial Services: Olivia Kindig Wells
Art Director: James Boone

Southern Living ANNUALS & PERENNIALS

Editor: Lois Trigg Chaplin
Assistant Editor: Kelly Hooper Troiano
Copy Editor: Keri Bradford Anderson
Editorial Assistants: Heather Averett, Robin Boteler
Garden Editor, *Southern Living*: Linda C. Askey
Indexer: Katharine R. Wiencke
Designer: Carol Loria
Senior Photographer, *Southern Living*: Van Chaplin
Director, Production and Distribution: Phillip Lee
Associate Production Manager:
Vanessa Cobbs Richardson
Production Assistant: Faye Porter Bonner

Our appreciation to the staff of *Southern Living*
magazine for their contributions to this book.

Cover: *Coreopsis and mealy-cup sage*
Frontispiece: *Spring border featuring
foxgloves, peonies, and sweet William*
Right: *Four o' clocks*

We're Here for You!
We at Oxmoor House are dedicated to serving you with reliable
information that expands your imagination and enriches your life.
We welcome your comments and suggestions. Please write to us at:

Oxmoor House, Inc.
Editor, *Annuals & Perennials*
2100 Lakeshore Drive
Birmingham, AL 35209

To order additional publications, call 1-205-877-6560.

Contents

Geranium

Lantana

Contents

Purslane

Spider flower

Butterfly weed

Phlox and bearded iris

Annuals and Perennials Primer

The lingering blooms of summer (lantana, pentas, cosmos, and Mexican heather) merge with the new blossoms of fall-blooming Mexican bush sage.

Paint a landscape for all seasons by planting varied combinations of annuals and perennials.

Brightening your landscape is as easy as adding a few spots of color with flowers. You can plant flowers in great sweeps of vivid color or place those of one delicate hue in single pots. You'll find hundreds of flowers available; their blooms range from whites to subtle pastels to bold, vibrant colors, and their foliage includes every shade of green. With the wealth of available choices of annuals and perennials, the possibilities for your garden are almost endless. But you don't need to spend hours working outdoors to add interest to your landscape. You just need to know a few basics about annuals and perennials in order to select the right plants for your particular site and climate.

Some annuals, such as these spider flowers, last until the first frost.

In the simplest of terms, an ***annual*** is a plant that sprouts, blooms, makes seed, and dies within a single year. But this in no way describes the versatility of these plants as they bring new color, new combinations, and new texture to a garden. The majority of annuals are planted in the spring, bloom through summer and fall, and are killed by frost. These are called ***warm-weather annuals*** and include such popular plants as impatiens, rose verbena, and globe amaranth. Other annuals are planted in fall or early spring and flower

Impatiens often self-sow, reappearing on their own from seed dropped the previous year.

ANNUALS THAT SEED THEMSELVES

Some annuals drop seeds as they mature. Then if the weather and soil in your garden are just right, new plants will appear the next year. This habit may fool you into thinking they are perennials, but they are not. They are simply annuals that reestablish themselves from seed as nature intended. The offspring may differ from the original in height and color, but such surprises are part of the fun of gardening. Here are a few annuals that reseed themselves.

Black-eyed Susan
Calliopsis
Cosmos
Four o'clock
Globe amaranth
Iceland poppy
Impatiens
Klondyke cosmos
Madagascar periwinkle
Marigold
Melampodium
Shirley poppy
Snow-on-the-mountain
Spider flower
Sunflower
Sweet pea
Zinnia

Annuals and Perennials Primer

Pansies in a strawberry jar provide color in fall, winter, and early spring.

through the cool months. These are *cool-weather annuals,* such as poppies, pansies, and sweet peas, all of which bloom until high temperatures cause their decline.

Compared to annuals, which live a year or less, *perennials* are more permanent components of your garden, lasting several years. Perennials provide repeated color, fragrance, and texture through the seasons, year after year. Most perennials have stems and foliage that are killed by cold or put to rest by summer heat, but their roots survive. These plants wax and wane on a seasonal clock, repeating the cycle for many years.

Perennials are not easily categorized, but most fit one or more of the following descriptions. *Half-hardy perennials,* such as azure sage, are perennial only in areas with mild winters; elsewhere they are grown as annuals. *Ephemeral perennials* may live a long time, but their blooms and foliage last only a short span each year. Virginia bluebells fall in this category; they come up, bloom, and disappear within three months. *Evergreen perennials,* such as hellebores and dianthus, are quite the opposite. They keep their leaves year-round and can serve as ground covers.

Autumn Joy sedum is one of the most popular fall-flowering perennials because of its many interesting changes in form and color from spring until winter.

A few perennials are *shrubby,* developing woody, shrublike stems; an example is tree peony. These perennials usually need pruning to keep them vigorous and full. ***Short-lived perennials,*** such as cardinal flower, last just two or three years and then must be replaced. Then, as their name suggests, ***long-lived perennials*** live for many years, sometimes decades. Peonies are among the most durable—they may even live long enough for several generations of a family to enjoy.

Because perennials grow for years, multiplying and spreading, you will probably share them by giving away pieces or divisions or by digging them up entirely. Iris, daisies, and mums are a few of the dozens of perennials that tend to multiply. (See pages 45 and 46 for more about propagating perennials.)

Unlike shrubs, which grow larger each year and eventually become too bulky to transplant, perennials allow you the freedom to rearrange and replace them. With perennials, you can easily yield to the temptation to move them (although a few may resist it). Transplant them to a spot where they look better, smell stronger, or appear brighter in combination with another plant. In fact, the fun of growing perennials is finding just the right spot where a plant looks best and then deciding which other plants should accompany it.

A final group of flowering plants you might find are ***biennials,*** which are usually sold with annuals. They do not behave like annuals or perennials. Instead, biennials typically live two years. In the first growing season, they produce plenty of foliage but no blooms; flowers appear the second year. If you sow the seeds in spring, the plants probably won't bloom until the second year. However, if you buy them at a garden center, they will have spent some time in a greenhouse; that means they will bloom the year you plant them as if they were annuals. Other biennials are hybridized to bloom in their first season, although they are botanically biennial. Three popular biennials are foxglove, hollyhock, and sweet William.

These pages offer you information and ideas for enjoying all types of flowers in your garden year-round. Read through the book for ideas; then adapt them to your plan. Experiment with new colors, designs, and combinations. Whatever selections of annuals and perennials you choose, you'll be able to create a garden that is truly your own.

Purple and orange coneflowers are tough, easy-to-grow perennials that brighten summer and fall gardens.

Flowers in the Landscape

Integrate flowers into the landscape to bring new color to the greens of trees and shrubs.

Flowers and their foliage offer a wealth of color and texture for all seasons.

Flowers have the quality gardeners value most—color. And that makes using them in the landscape one of the most rewarding aspects of gardening. Like decorating with color indoors, placing color in the garden with plants requires careful planning and involves trial and error. However, flowers are forgiving. If you plant perennials and then decide you don't like where they are, you can always dig them up and move them to a better location. Or you may find that you don't like the color of an annual you planted. If so, just pick out another color the following year. Flowers offer you flexibility in the garden—so take advantage of it and try new things. Plant flowers in a simple single clump in a pot, as part of a formal, full-blown English-style border, or in any arrangement you want to create. Flowers are so varied that the possibilities are almost limitless.

These pages give you ideas for placing flowers in your garden in relation to other flowers and other types of plants. Study the photographs for inspiration, and then experiment with different colors and types of plants in your own garden.

Planning Your Flowerbeds

Bring color, texture, and seasonal interest to your garden by arranging plants in planned groups. Plant annuals and perennials in large or small beds or even in containers. Whatever physical requirements your landscape dictates, you can make the most of your flowers by planning a color scheme.

Masses of Color in Large Beds

Group flowers in a bed to create a swath of uniform color or texture, or intermingle them with other blocks of color. Dense color masses spread over a large area can make quite an impact, especially when viewed from a distance.

Blend different types of flowers for an interplay of color while the seasons change, or plant a single type for consistent, season-long color. Too many contrasting plants can result in a jumbled horticultural "zoo," but you can add unity and rhythm to your landscape by using masses of a reasonable number of species or selections.

Annuals. When setting out annuals in large masses, plant an entire flat or more of the same variety together in gentle curves. This is most effective with pansies, Madagascar periwinkle, narrow-leaf zinnias, and other plants that knit together to create a "carpet."

For the most striking show, make your beds at least 3 feet wide, preferably wider, and as long as your back and budget allow. You may even want some beds to extend the length of the property. When using groups of annuals as part of a tapestry of many colors, plant enough of the same plant, usually 3 to 10, to make a respectable group.

Swamp sunflower and Mexican bush sage bring color to the garden in late summer and early fall.

Repeated masses of color, such as these yellow pansies, provide continuity in a flowerbed containing foxgloves, sweet William, and other plants.

Flowers in the Landscape

A classic border often follows a color theme, such as that of pastels. However, the look of the border will change from season to season as flowers reach their seasonal peaks and give way to other plants. These midspring blooms include foxgloves, poppies, sweet William, and begonias.

Hostas and ajuga combine to make an impressive ground cover.

Perennials. Large perennial beds and the mix of flowers within them define a classic English treatment called a ***border.*** For an effective border, be sure to provide a strong background to help the plants stand out. Plan a color theme such as pastels, bright colors, or all white. Choose plants with as much seasonal variety as possible, and the border will show off year-round color. Annuals can bloom for months; use them to fill color gaps between the waxing and waning of perennials. Then the border will always have something to offer during each season.

Make your border at least 6 feet deep (10 feet is even better) to allow plenty of room for combining annuals and perennials successfully. The border can be as long as your space, time, and money allow. The classic border treatment also involves a fair amount of shoveling, as you may change the initial placement of plants when you experiment with what looks good in your landscape.

A few perennials are sturdy enough to use as ***ground covers.*** Many of these spread to blanket the ground with handsome evergreen foliage so that the plants look good even when not in bloom. Evergreen daylilies and hellebores are excellent choices. Perennials used in this manner require a bit more maintenance than do typical ground covers; you may need to divide them to rejuvenate the planting.

Spots of Color in the Garden

Many of your flowers may end up in small beds because of your time or space requirements. In this case, remember that flowers attract the eye. Use the spots of color strategically for accents, and always place them where you want people to look. Do not plant colorful flowers to hide the air-conditioning unit or another eyesore; flowers simply draw more attention to it. Instead, use flowers to mark the entrance to your home, the foot of a fountain or a birdbath, a patio cutout, or any other carefully identified spaces.

Clumps of Japanese roof iris, white bearded iris, and pink peony are all that are needed in this small flowerbed. After the blooms fade, the foliage will remain handsome for months.

Annuals. Spots of color call for an annual that looks good for the longest possible time, such as Madagascar periwinkle, impatiens, wax begonia, or melampodium. Annuals also work well when used to fill in between perennials and shrubs in a bed. Because they bloom for months, their color is a constant you can count on as other plants fade. Annuals are also a nice tool for unifying a mixed planting. Try repeating one or two types throughout a bed to bring unity.

PRACTICAL POINTERS

• Put the tallest plants toward the back of a bed, or plant them in the center of a bed that will be viewed from all sides.

• Remember plant compatibility. What makes the plants you choose grow best: sun or shade, wet or dry soil? Do not mix plants with opposite needs, or your bed will have a ragged appearance as one plant thrives and another struggles.

• When mixing flowers with other plants, do not plant just one unless it is a very large plant, such as Mexican bush sage or lantana. Instead, plant in groups of three or five. Place plants so that they form an equilateral triangle or a sweep. They will grow together to make one clump, which will have more visual impact than a single plant.

• When planning a large flowerbed, design it to be viewed down its length. It will look more lush and full.

Red geraniums lend spots of color to an evergreen entry.

Flowers in the Landscape

Coneflowers brighten a green garden whose show otherwise depends on the contrast of leaf textures.

Perennials. Often we think of perennials in only one form—a large border. However, the majority of perennials serve as plants in small flowerbeds. This is especially effective when perennials are paired with annuals that will fill the void when the perennials are not in bloom. Place small flowerbeds in the corner of a landscape, between a walkway and a wall, beside a patio, or in a courtyard. When planning a small bed, it is critical to choose perennials that look good for a long time, such as Goldsturm coneflower, yarrow, showy sedum, salvia, and coreopsis. If the bed is in a prominent spot, provide the perennials with some evergreen accompaniment, such as a small boxwood.

Specialty Gardens

In garden borders and massed plantings, annuals and perennials can provide everything from a subdued range of delicate hues to a riot of brilliant color. Blend different types of flowers for an interplay of color, or create a garden with a very specific purpose. The planting and care of a specialty garden may take more time than a small bed or even a larger one that contains a limited number of selections. However, the pleasure it brings outweighs the difficulties.

Blue phlox and bearded iris, a good pair of spring perennials, complement each other both in color and form.

KEEP A GARDEN JOURNAL

Keep a notebook to jot down selections of plants that pleased you so that you will be sure to buy them again. Record those that did not work well to avoid future disappointment. Include notes on planting dates, disease or insect problems and solutions, length of bloom, cold hardiness, tolerance of rainy weather, and anything else that will help you next time around. If you purchased a plant from a mail-order source, note the name of the company to remind yourself where to order additional plants at a later date.

Cutting gardens. The ideal way to grow flowers for cutting is to plant a garden that is set apart from the landscape. Plant the cutting garden in rows instead of in groups arranged by color and size, and do not be concerned about clashing colors or plant heights. This format lets you replace plants as they wane without upsetting the layout; it also provides extra space between plants so that the flowers can grow large and their stems strong. Plants crammed close together in a flower border are not the best flowers for cutting; crowding makes the stems thin and weak.

This cutting garden provides sunflowers, zinnias, and other blooms to bring indoors.

Cottage gardens. These are one of today's most popular garden styles. They date back to a time when landscaping and garden design were hardly priorities. The original cottage gardeners used plants they already had or were given, or they started plants from seed. They did not always place them according to strict design principles; many plants grew where they seeded themselves.

You can achieve a cottage garden-style flowerbed with many of the old-fashioned flowers easily started from seed. Starting from seed is less expensive than buying transplants, but it requires more patience as you nurture seedlings and control weeds. (See pages 37 through 39 for more about sowing seed.)

Another common way to add to your cottage garden is to start new plants from existing perennials. Most perennials actually need thinning or dividing in order to bloom better, so your friends and neighbors will appreciate your request to divide and transplant a favorite perennial. (See pages 45 and 46 for more information on propagating perennials.)

Shade gardens. You may think of most flowers as flourishing more in the sun than in the shade, but many perennials thrive in areas that receive little sun. If you want an easy, relatively carefree way to bring color to shady areas, plant perennials. Many of the perennials suited to a shady garden are native wildflowers. They can carpet the periphery of a walkway or enliven the large, mulched shady areas of suburban lots. Perennials such as hellebore, a classic for shade, also make sturdy evergreen ground covers that bring winter color to

These zinnias and spider flowers were started from seed in early summer and reached full bloom within ten weeks.

Caladium and impatiens are both so dependable for shade that they have become a standard combination for areas under spreading trees.

wooded settings. Only a few annuals thrive in shade, but a mix of caladiums and impatiens will brighten any shady spot.

Butterfly and hummingbird gardens. Create a feeding ground for butterflies and hummingbirds by selecting annuals and perennials that attract these creatures. The larger the garden, the more effective it is. Butterfly and hummingbird gardens demand full sun and include in their flower mix bright red, orange, and yellow blooms. To be especially attractive to butterflies, your garden should include plants on which they lay their eggs, such as butterfly weed, hollyhocks, and parsley. Some choice flowers to attract adult butterflies are listed in the box below.

The butterfly garden at the Biltmore House in Asheville, North Carolina, is typical of this type of garden, with its brightly colored plants that attract butterflies and hummingbirds.

FLOWERS FOR BUTTERFLIES

To attract butterflies to your garden, plant these flowers. Use them together in large masses and in full sun, where butterflies prefer to feed.

Bee balm	Lantana
Butterfly bush	Purple coneflower
Butterfly weed	Sedum
Globe amaranth	Verbena
Joe-pye weed	Zinnia

Color in Containers

Growing flowers in containers allows you to put color right where you want it. Typical places include patios, decks, and window boxes, but you can even move pots indoors for a temporary decoration. The bright blooms bring instant color indoors. Containers also provide a simple way to maintain color outdoors at minimal expense, even if you have not planted a formal garden. Flowers planted in containers do need more water than those planted in the ground. Water container plants every day if they are outdoors during hot weather; water frequently if they are indoors.

Pots. Pots are easier to reach and maintain than garden beds, and they require fewer tools. Mix annuals in a large pot to provide a variety of color and form. Pair upright plants, such as geraniums or dusty miller, with cascading ones like petunias, sweet alyssum, or purslane. Good perennials for pots are evergreens, such as Bath's Pink; its soft pink blooms and fine-textured leaves will cascade gracefully over the edge of a container. Or look for plants that put on a display for many weeks, such as showy sedum or hosta.

You can also plan a succession of potted flowers year-round by choosing several that bloom in different seasons and by planting them in small plastic containers. When one plant is in bloom, slip the plastic pot into a decorative clay one; replace with another plant in bloom when the show has faded.

Mix annuals and perennials in a large pot to provide a variety of color and form. Pair upright plants, such as iris, with cascading ones, such as candytuft. When planting perennials, choose evergreens with contrasting foliage so that they will look good when not in bloom.

Hanging baskets. Another popular type of container is the hanging basket, which allows plants to dangle. Use special stands to hold a collection of baskets, or hang baskets from eaves, arbors, upper porch rails—almost anywhere. To dress up your home instantly, purchase matching hanging baskets and remove the hangers. Place each basket in a terra-cotta or other type of pot for a welcoming arrangement of color.

Window boxes. This type of container brings your flowers into perfect view from indoors. Always popular for the front of the house, window boxes are ideal for the window of a child's room or that of a housebound person. A window box provides a wonderful way to enjoy various annuals and perennials each season.

Showy sedum looks good at many stages of its growth cycle. It is quite drought tolerant, which makes it a good choice for a container.

This basket combines roselike double impatiens with the foliage of asparagus fern and variegated ivy.

A colorful mix of petunias, asters, artemisia, veronica, bacopa, marigolds, and asparagus fern makes an attractive window box.

Repetition of colors and plants creates harmony. Pansies in yellow and blue along with pink geraniums fill in the spaces between perennial candytuft, peonies, and iris.

Colors and Combinations

You will enjoy your garden most when you use flowers and foliage to paint a picture that changes with the seasons. Translating a rainbow of flowers into an orchestrated design calls for a careful study of the plants available to you. Approach color and texture combinations as if you were decorating a room. A little planning helps when planting a flower garden.

Start with the Color Wheel

While selecting color is a matter of personal taste, the color wheel on this page shows how colors naturally work together. The wheel is an artist's tool for previewing the impact of certain color combinations and helps simplify color selection.

Primary colors. To use this color wheel, cut a small equilateral triangle of paper and position it on the wheel so that its points are on the three primary colors—red, yellow, and blue. All other colors are produced by a mixture of these three. If mixed in equal amounts, primary colors produce the secondary colors: orange comes from a mixture of yellow and red; green from yellow and blue; and violet from red and blue.

As you rotate the triangle, its points show trios of colors at equidistances on the wheel. These colors will work well together, making it easy for you to group flowers of corresponding colors.

Complementary colors. The colors directly opposite one another on the color wheel are complementary. They are also called high-contrast colors because they create a strong contrast when paired together, yet they

Color Wheel

red
red violet
red orange
violet
orange
blue violet
yellow orange
blue
yellow
blue green
yellow green
green

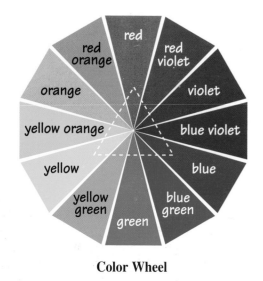

Yellow always complements blue or purple flowers. These yellow daffodils bring the purple pansies to life.

A harmonious mix of related shades of pansies and phlox creates a soft, unified planting.

still present a pleasing combination. To achieve dramatic effects in your garden, plant red geraniums against a green backdrop or create a border of yellow tulips underplanted with deep blue pansies.

Harmonious colors. These are the colors that are close to one another on the color wheel. They all share some mix of the three primary colors or have the same hue. For example, a combination of deep blue, blue violet, and lavender flowers creates a softly harmonious garden.

Warm and cool colors. Another method of organization on the color wheel is the separation of warm and cool colors. Warm colors are inherently vibrant and visible; cool colors are soothing and create a feeling of serenity.

Identify warm and cool colors on the color wheel by drawing a dividing line between the red and red violet on one side and the green and yellow-green on the other. The warm tones center around orange, and the cool tones are around blue. You can create some interesting contrasts by pairing a warm tone with a cool one, such as yellow coreopsis and the deep purple mealy-cup sage.

Plan Color in Your Garden

When planning your garden, consider the color of your home and the surrounding areas. For instance, red brick does not make a good backdrop for red flowers, but red blooms are exquisite against a gray wall or sidewalk. Turn the page for some ideas on employing the colors of annuals and perennials in your landscape design.

Evergreen trees and shrubs provide a rich background for flowers. Here snapdragons do indeed snap against the dark evergreens.

A Few Good Combinations

Quiet

Bachelor's button
  and pale pink sweet William

Blue pansy
  and white evergreen candytuft

Dusty miller and blue ageratum

Pale pink sweet William
  and white pansy

Lavender iris and pale pink dianthus

Vibrant

Blue pansy and yellow pansy

Blue pansy and yellow daffodil

Dark pink snapdragon
  and deep yellow coreopsis

Hot pink petunia and orange marigold

Scarlet sage
  and Mexican mint marigold

Showy sedum
  and orange narrow-leaf zinnia

Yellow daylilies
  and magenta dwarf globe amaranth

Chartreuse hostas
  and dwarf mondo grass

Flowers in the Landscape

Most flowers stand out against a dark background. Here coreopsis is accompanied by the globes of allium (a bulb) in front of a hedge.

Start with green. For a successful foreground of flowers, you need a background of green. Evergreen shrubs are especially nice during the winter months because they provide constant foliage if the bed is otherwise dormant.

Punctuate with color. The use of color for bold accents is limited only by your imagination. Consider placing a spot of strong color near an entryway to define it and attract attention; if you have a primarily evergreen garden, use color in pots or beds to enliven the green.

Use colors to impart mood. The warm colors—red, orange, and bright yellow—attract attention by suggesting both sunshine and flame. They make a garden happy and lively and can also make it warm and cozy.

Such colors become good choices for the winter and early spring garden but are perhaps less appealing for summer, when warmth is not needed. In contrast, white, blue, and pastel flowers seem cooler and are pleasant choices for a tree-shaded spot in the summertime. Many people prefer soft, quiet colors for formal gardens where evergreens and a sculpture, topiary, or water feature are the main attractions.

Petunias, annual phlox, and verbena in shades of purple, red, and deep pink combine with yellow sedum to give this bed a warm glow in early spring.

Use color to control space. Warm-colored blooms attract your eye and stand out against the background. They are more noticeable and tend to come forward in the landscape. They shrink the space between the plant and your eye, making a large garden feel smaller and more intimate. On the other hand, the cool colors—especially blue and violet—tend to recede, creating the perception of depth. And just as light-colored walls open up a space, so do pale blooms.

Use color to unify. Repeat one shade of blooms, such as white or pale lavender, to unify an assortment of brightly colored flowers.

Use white for nighttime enjoyment. White is not only striking but also clearly visible under moonlight or outdoor lighting. The most effective white flowers are flat blooms, such as those of moonflower and single peonies. Light-colored foliage, such as the large leaves of white caladiums or chartreuse hostas, also shows up well after dark. Because nighttime is often the only opportunity you have to enjoy a deck or patio, always consider white flowers for at least one spot in your garden.

Use blue liberally for various effects. Create excitement by pairing color-wheel opposites, such as blue with orange or yellow. For a quieter mood, combine blue with white, silver, or violet; these shades emphasize the coolness of blue.

Pale colors of impatiens, geraniums, and petunias were carefully chosen for this courtyard to help create a sense of spaciousness and distance.

A spot of yellow pansies and deep pink tulips adds color to a quiet combination of white azaleas, woodland phlox, and purple pansies.

Flowers in the Landscape

To combine plants that will complement each other, you should know as much about each plant as possible. Here are some questions to ask that will help you pair plants with compatible growth habits, bloom times, form, and horticultural requirements.

How tall and wide will it grow?

What shape and color are the flowers?

How long does it bloom?

When does it bloom?

Does the foliage stay green through winter?

Does it spread?

Does it form clumps?

Does it like sun or shade?

Will it tolerate poor soil or bad drainage?

A chartreuse hosta provides excellent textural contrast with English ivy, sweet woodruff, another hosta, and acanthus.

Don't Forget the Foliage

Some flowers, such as the silver-leafed dusty miller, are as prized for their foliage as they are for their flowers. Others, such as coleus or hostas, are grown solely for the widely varied colors of their leaves. These plants can lift a bed from ordinary to extraordinary by giving you a surprise: just when you expect flowers, leaves instead create the show. The chartreuse foliage of some selections of coleus and hosta contrasts vividly with deep-colored flowers, and the dark green or maroon types of coleus are a perfect foil for vibrant and pale pinks.

Chartreuse coleus is just one annual with unusual colored leaves that are as showy as a flower.

The silver leaves of dusty miller make these yellow iris pop.

The silver foliage of dusty miller or of fuzzy lamb's ears is every bit as showy as a flower, if not more so. The silvery white leaves beckon from a distance and shimmer in sunlight and moonlight. Use silver to enhance any color; it provides a gentle backdrop to the richness of purple globe amaranth, orange marigolds, and other pale or bright flowers. Mix silvery foliage with green-leafed plants, such as the fan-shaped bearded iris, to create a stunning effect. Like white flowers, silver foliage is more prominent at night than is green foliage.

Finally, consider using plants with variegated foliage. This foliage is the hallmark of snow-on-the-mountain as well as several selections of coleus and hosta. Such foliage becomes an accent when surrounded by darker leaves and enlivens any nearby flowers with its contrasting colors. Use the colors of the foliage of annuals, shrubs, and other perennials to enhance the show.

The purple leaves of Setcreasea purpurea *repeat the color of Japanese iris. The composition is sparked by yellow coreopsis (right) and yarrow (left) with white calla lily peeping through.*

Plantings for Each Season

Spring and fall offer the widest variety of blooming plants, but you can plan around the seasons to keep yearlong color in your garden. The photos on these pages show some colorful examples of seasonal blooms. The reward comes in mixing annuals that overlap the seasons with perennials and shrubs that may bloom for only a short time. Annuals provide long-lasting sweeps of vivid color that you can change from year to year, while your perennials will reappear for several years.

◀ *Spring: This spring array in shades of pink, purple, and white includes iris, daisies, chives, petunias, sweet William, and pansies.*

▲ **Spring to Fall:** *Caladiums, mealy-cup sage, coleus, and white impatiens provide months of color on this terrace from spring until frost strikes in the fall.*

Summer: ▶
A small monument is the focus of this summer garden of lamb's ears and yellow yarrow.

Flowers in the Landscape

▼ *Summer to Fall: Narrow-leaf zinnia, mealy-cup sage, and white impatiens linger from summer into fall to mix with the autumn tones of perennial Autumn Joy sedum as it comes into bloom.*

◀ **Fall:** *This fall garden includes chrysanthemums, showy sedum, coneflowers, salvia, and the annual narrow-leaf zinnia.*

▼ **Winter:** *Bearsfoot hellebore is treasured for its flowers and evergreen foliage during winter.*

Getting Started

Purchase annuals from a reliable garden center where transplants such as these caladiums and impatiens are carefully tended.

Start with healthy plants and sound knowledge about planting and caring for your flowers.

Planning ahead is the key to growing beautiful flowers. Before investing a lot of time and money in your garden, learn about purchasing plants, preparing the soil, and proper planting methods. The result will be flowers that will reward you now and for years to come.

Consumer Horticulture

When you shop for groceries, you probably enter the supermarket with a good idea of what you need to buy. When you visit the garden center or order flowers from a mail-order source, you should do the same. Know how many plants you need to start a bed and whether you want to start with transplants or from seed. Be familiar with the form in which the plant is sold. Annuals are generally sold as transplants and from seed. Garden centers usually sell perennials in containers; mail-order sources often ship them **bare root,** that is, without soil on their roots.

Working with Transplants

Transplants are seedlings that have been grown in small pots to be planted late in the garden. They give you a head start over seeding directly in the garden and are usually more dependable than seed. Often many of the varieties sold as transplants are difficult to start from seed at home. The most economical way to purchase transplants is in flats that hold **cell packs,** small plastic "four-packs" or "six-packs" of plants.

Use the Plant Purchasing Guide below to determine how many plants you need per square foot of garden. Read the label to find the recommended spacing for your plant. Multiply the number of plants needed per square foot by the number of square feet in your bed. This is the total number of plants you need to purchase.

Example: A bed 6 feet deep and 10 feet wide has 60 square feet of planting area. If the label recommends spacing the plants 8 inches apart, then multiply 2.6 times 60 for a total of 156 plants to fill the bed.

Bedding plants, such as these petunias (left) and geraniums (right), come in flats that should be watered thoroughly before the plants are removed.

Annuals. Smaller plants are ideal for planting early in the season when there is adequate time for them to grow. Most annuals grow very fast, often reaching their mature size within 8 to 12 weeks after planting.

Most flats of bedding plants hold 24 to 48 plants, depending on the size of the packs. Packs may have three, four, or six cells each. Water a flat thoroughly before removing the transplants for planting. If transplants are even slightly dry, they may be difficult to water properly once planted.

Flats may also contain plants grown in 4-inch pots. Four-inch pots come 16 to a flat, with one plant per pot. The larger size of these plants is an advantage if you are planting them late in the growing season. As the season progresses, nurseries sometimes sell large, mature annuals in 8-inch and gallon-sized containers. You can plant these for instant color. However, if planted late in the season, transplants require very diligent watering to ease their transition from pot to ground.

PLANT PURCHASING GUIDE

Spacing Between Plants	Plants per Square Foot
6 inches	4.41
8 inches	2.60
10 inches	1.66
12 inches	1.15
15 inches	0.738
18 inches	0.512
24 inches	0.290

The label tells you that these young green petunia plants will bear white blooms.

Look for well-developed white fibrous roots, a sign of a healthy plant.

It is best to buy transplants that have not yet started blooming. Older plants in small cells often have become **root bound.** This means that their roots have formed an impenetrable mat and may be growing through the holes at the bottom of the container. Ideally, you want to plant a young green plant and give it a chance to develop plenty of new foliage before it begins to bloom. Although purchasing transplants before they bloom does not allow you to see the color of the flowers, these younger plants transplant with the least shock; those that are large and root bound need extra care.

Perennials. Perennials grown in containers are ready to be planted directly in the garden. Most of these plants come in larger pots. Because perennials live for a long time, they are likely to remain in the pot for a while; this gives them a chance to grow. Some gallon-sized plants may be a year old when you buy them; the larger size of these plants is an advantage if you plant them late in the growing season.

As with annuals, the most economical way to purchase perennials is as young transplants—in cell packs, in 4-inch pots, or bare root. Sometimes a few perennials, such as evergreen candytuft, dianthus, and Shasta daisies, are sold in the smaller cell packs. If you are buying potted perennials to create a mass planting, such as for a ground cover, you will need quite a few plants. Many of the best buys are in 4-inch pots; those plants are generally large enough for good growth the first season and cost less than do the 1-gallon plants.

Bare-root perennials should come packed in damp peat moss or sawdust so that their roots remain moist. Plant them soon after they arrive, first soaking the roots for a few hours.

Selecting Healthy Plants

Check that each cell in the flat contains a healthy plant. If foliage appears mottled, look at the underside of the leaves for aphids, whiteflies, or spider mites. If the transplants appear weak, slip one out of the pack to check the roots. Healthy roots are white and fibrous; soft or brown roots are a sign of disease.

It is also crucial that you purchase transplants that have received proper care. Those that spend days baking in a sidewalk display and are allowed to severely wilt between waterings will not grow into healthy plants.

Buying Seed

Some plants, such as cosmos and spider flower, are rarely found as transplants because they grow unwieldy very quickly. To grow them, you must purchase seed from either a garden center or a mail-order seed company and start your own transplants indoors or sow seed directly in the garden. Likewise, to save money, you can start a few perennials, such as evergreen candytuft, from seed either in the garden or indoors. (See page 38 for more about starting seed indoors.) Just remember that starting from seed is more economical than buying transplants only if you do it right.

Always buy seed dated for the current year, and only purchase packets that have been properly stored in a cool, dry environment. Packets that are wrinkled with moisture or left sitting in the sun may contain seed that has lost its viability.

Buying Bulbs and Tubers

Some bulbs are sold only at specific times of the year, so it pays to shop early for the best selection, even if it is not time to plant. In the South, Dutch bulbs, such as tulips, are sold in September, but the best time to plant them is after the first frost. The bulblike tubers for caladiums and other summer plants arrive at the nursery in March. However, they prefer warm soil, so you should plant them in April or May—or at least two weeks after the last frost.

Storing Transplants and Seed

When you cannot plant everything the day you bring it home, keep the plants and seeds in top condition until you can get them in the ground. Place transplants outdoors in partial shade with protection from afternoon sun, and water daily if needed. If they sit for more than two weeks, water with a diluted liquid fertilizer, such as fish emulsion or commercial houseplant fertilizer. Try to plant transplants within a week or two to keep the plants from becoming root bound and stunted.

Store unused seeds in a sealed plastic container in the refrigerator or freezer. Never leave seeds in an outdoor storage room or any place where they might be exposed to water or humidity. Bulbs and tubers are much hardier, and most do well if stored in a cool, dry place until you are ready to place them in the ground.

PLANTS THAT ARE EASY TO START FROM SEED

Calliopsis	Marigold
Candytuft	Morning glory
Coreopsis	Spider flower
Cosmos	Sunflower
Four o'clock	Sweet pea
Globe amaranth	Zinnia

Keep seed packets, bulbs, and tubers in a cool, dry place until planting time. Plant these caladium tubers in mid- to late spring.

Good soil preparation is a key to successful flowerbeds.

Breaking Ground

The flowers you plant are only as good as the conditions you provide for them. Granted, some plants tolerate neglect better than others, but all do best with some basic care. If you give them the right amount of sunlight, good soil, and proper watering and feeding, they will grow larger and bear more flowers than poorly tended plants.

Prepare the Planting Bed

The ideal soil is loose enough to allow roots to expand easily and is porous, well drained, and able to retain moisture and nutrients. But such soil is rarely found naturally around your home. You must create your own by adding wheelbarrow loads of organic matter, such as compost, manure, or sphagnum peat moss. Organic matter improves clay soil by opening it up so that roots can breathe and drain properly. It also helps poor, sandy soil hold more moisture and nutrients.

When possible, begin preparing your soil a couple of weeks before planting. Then you can do the job in stages rather than all at once. If the spot has never been cultivated, begin by removing anything growing there. You can transplant healthy grass to bare spots elsewhere in the yard or spray the entire area with a nonselective herbicide to kill existing grass and weeds. These products will kill everything green that they touch, so follow label directions carefully. A few days after spraying, break up the dead vegetation with a turning fork or tiller and remove it to a compost pile.

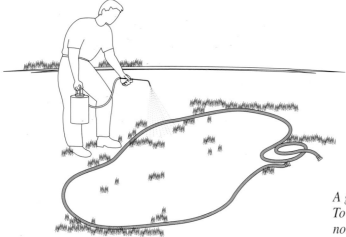

A garden hose helps define the outline of a new flowerbed. To kill grass and weeds within the outline, spray with a nonselective herbicide a week or two before turning the soil.

Use a turning fork to work the soil as deeply as possible, preferably 12 to 18 inches in heavy clay. Rent a tiller for large beds. Make sure the soil is not wet when you work with it; otherwise, it will dry in clods. Spread a layer of organic matter 3 to 4 inches deep over the area; work it with your fork or tiller until well blended with the native soil. Each time you work organic matter into the soil it becomes softer, making your work easier.

If you need to add lime to reduce the acid in the soil (raise the pH level), do this as soon as possible. Often the most practical time to add lime is when you first till the bed. However, it takes weeks for pulverized lime to raise the soil's pH level, so you may want to use hydrated lime, which acts more quickly. Because this type is also more caustic, follow label precautions carefully.

When you till is also a convenient time to add fertilizer, working it into the soil at the same time that you do the lime.

Spread a layer of organic matter to work into the bed before setting plants. This is also a good time to add lime, if needed, and starter fertilizer.

Till the bed to incorporate the organic matter, fertilizer, and lime (if needed) at least 8 inches into the soil.

HINTS FOR BREAKING NEW GROUND

• When testing your soil, take samples from different parts of the area to get an accurate reading.

• Mark the outline of a new bed by stretching a garden hose out in the shape of the bed (see facing page), or draw the proposed edges with spray paint. The lines will help you keep your grass-and-weed killer within bounds.

• Never work the soil when it is wet, as it will dry in clods. However, tilling is easier if the soil is slightly moist, especially heavy clay soil. Water the day before tilling, or plan your project to follow a light rain.

Collect soil samples to test pH and levels of plant nutrients present in your soil.

Always Do a Soil Test

To know how to treat your soil, you need to assess your soil's chemistry. Is the soil's acid level (pH) too high or low? How much nitrogen, phosphorus, and potassium does it need? In certain areas of the country, salt levels are high; in others, the native soil may be deficient of a crucial element. A soil test will tell you what your soil needs.

You can get soil test kits through your county Extension Service office. The kit contains directions for testing, along with a form to record your findings. Most states charge a small fee, but it is well worth the cost to determine exactly what your soil needs to yield beautiful, healthy plants.

Ensure Good Drainage

The most common cause of problems with flowers is a poorly drained planting site. There are a few plants, such as cannas, that do not mind soggy soil, but most need good drainage to avoid root rot. If you cannot plant on a site that drains well, build a raised bed for your plants. See the box below for information on how to build one.

ABOUT RAISED BEDS

You can raise the level of the soil to improve drainage by building a bed on top of the ground. Till the native soil as if preparing it for planting. This helps the soil in the raised area drain into the ground below.

Build a raised bed by simply mounding the soil about a foot high or by building a box from landscape timbers, mortared brick, or stacked stone. When filling the raised bed, incorporate native soil along with compost in the soil mix. (Do not include native soil if you have had problems with plants rotting at the base or roots or if plants have been stunted by nematodes.)

Prepare the soil for raised beds as you would for any other type bed.

A raised bed improves drainage on low ground.

Planting

Once you prepare your beds, you're ready to set out seed, bulbs or tubers, and transplants. Just remember that proper planting of these is essential to the success of your flowers. They will be healthier and more vigorous if they get a good start, which includes everything from the way you handle the plants to the soil in which they grow.

Handling Young Plants

When you bring transplants home, keep them watered and in light shade until planting time. Try to get them into the ground within a few days after purchasing.

Remove a transplant from its pot by turning the pot upside down and sliding the plant out. Never pull it by the stem, or you may tear it from its roots. Handle young plants gently.

Sometimes you have no choice but to purchase plants that are a bit root bound. This is common with ageratum, marigolds, pansies, and globe amaranth. In this case, gently score the roots with a sharp knife, making one vertical cut just through the surface on each side of the root ball. For plants with large roots, such as hostas and daylilies, simply take your finger and gently pull a few away from the tangled mass. These procedures will help the roots grow out of the mass and into their new bed. Otherwise, the tangled roots will stay exactly the size they were when planted, and the plant will not grow.

Perhaps the step you will find most difficult is this last one: remove the flowers from your young transplants when you plant them. They need to grow larger before beginning to produce flowers; the bigger and leafier the plant is, the more it will bloom. Simply pinch off large flowers, such as marigolds, or snip smaller blooms, such as sweet alyssum, with scissors. To help keep the plants active, fertilize with a liquid plant food, such as 20-20-20, immediately after planting.

If you have ordered bare-root perennials, plant while they are dormant; this gives the roots a chance to become established before new growth begins in spring. Bare-root perennials that are shipped too late—after their tops have begun to sprout—need extra water and shade to ensure their survival in the garden. If possible, buy from a mail-order source whose shipping schedule coincides with your local planting dates, usually when deciduous trees are still bare.

Choose healthy plants that have not yet filled their containers with a network of roots.

Overgrown, root-bound transplants, such as these marigolds, need their roots untangled so that they will grow into the ground. Snip off blooms to help plants grow larger before blooming again.

Arrange larger plants before planting to give you a glimpse of how they will look next to each other. By doing this, you will be able to make changes more easily.

Setting Plants in the Bed

Always set a plant at the same depth it was planted in its original container. The top of the root ball should be level with the surface of the soil. It is more difficult to gauge the proper planting depth with bare-root plants. If you look carefully, you can sometimes see a soil line (a dirty or dark band of color) on the plants. If this is not visible, plant so that the *crown*—the point where the plant's top growth originates—sits just above soil level. Pat the soil around the plants firmly, but do not pack it down. The idea is to eliminate air pockets, while making sure that the root ball is in firm contact with the soil.

Space transplants according to the directions on the label. Although spacing is never exact and varies among selections of the same flower, plants placed too close together will compete for space. This causes their stems to grow spindly as they stretch for light. Rely on your own experience from working with different plants. Or read the plant label—it offers you accurate spacing information because it is selection specific. If plants are not labeled, shop where they are.

Press transplants firmly into the soil.

Plants have traits specific to each selection that affect their successful placement. Label plants in the garden, too, especially if you are planting new selections.

When planting several flats of plants, place plants in a staggered grid pattern rather than in even rows. This pattern ensures proper spacing and gives the bed a more organized look.

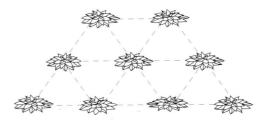

For a mass planting, plant in a diamond-grid pattern to achieve a more uniform look.

Seeding Directly in the Garden

Sowing seeds directly in the garden has several advantages: it involves less work than starting your own transplants, it costs less, and the seedlings do not suffer transplant shock.

To prepare the soil for seeding, loosen it with a turning fork or a tiller just as you would to set out transplants. Work plenty of organic matter into the bed. It is also crucial that you rake the ground, making it level and smooth so that the seeds will stay in place. Poke large seeds, such as sunflower seeds, gently into the ground at half the recommended spacing.

After the seedlings are 2 to 3 inches high, thin to the recommended spacing so that they are not too crowded. Plant at the recommended depth or slightly more shallow. It is better to plant slightly shallow than too deep—seeds that are buried too deep will not germinate.

Try to scatter seeds so that they fall about three times closer than the recommended spacing. Spread smaller seeds over the entire bed; then press them firmly into the soil. Do not bury them; instead, press them into the soil with the back of your hand, fingers together, or walk on a piece of plywood placed over the seeded area.

Water the seedlings. The key to raising seedlings is water. *Never* let the soil dry out. Use a mister or a fine sprinkler nozzle on your garden hose to keep the area moist. Water once a day until the seedlings are 1 to 2 inches tall; then water frequently enough to keep the soil moist but not soggy.

Thin the seedlings. Finally, be sure to thin seedlings as soon as the first true leaves appear. The first two leaves that poke through the ground are not true leaves but rather **cotyledons,** or seedling leaves, which provide energy. The next pair to appear are the true leaves, the first leaves that are shaped like those of a mature plant, only smaller. They are usually visible within a week after sprouting. Thin seedlings to half the recommended spacing at first, and then thin again a week or two later to the spacing recommended on the seed packet.

Flowers whose seeds germinate quickly are easy to start directly in the garden.

Place seedlings in a sunny window or under a plant light so that they will develop properly. Without enough light, they will be weak and spindly.

Starting Seed Indoors

One of the advantages to growing your own transplants is that you can grow selections that are not available locally. Sometimes this is the only way to have the plants that you want. However, some perennials grown from seed may not bloom until the second or third year.

Growing annual transplants from seed is more dependable; it also allows you to time your plantings just when you want them, without relying upon the availability at the garden center. This is especially nice for fall-planted annuals, such as poppies.

Seed-Starting Tips

• The seeds of most flowers will germinate at a soil temperature of 65 to 70 degrees. This temperature is easy to achieve indoors, away from cold drafts and windows. You can place the seeded flat on top of the refrigerator or water heater until the seeds sprout.

• Use soil mixes for starting seed; they are both sterile and lightweight, allowing easy germination. Some contain a starter fertilizer to boost growth. Do not use garden soil; it may contain fungi or bacteria that cause plant diseases.

• Allow six weeks for seedlings to germinate. Time the seed sowing by counting back six weeks from the earliest date you can transplant. After that time, you can move them outdoors where they will both strengthen and grow more quickly.

• Fertilize weekly with a half-strength solution of liquid fertilizer, such as 20-20-20, before transplanting. Ideally, plants should be 3 to 4 inches tall and have sturdy stems and well-formed roots when transplanted.

• Seedlings need cool nighttime temperatures (60 to 65 degrees); high nighttime temperatures may cause spindly growth.

A SEED-STARTING SUPPLY LIST

Seeds
Seed-starting container
Sterile seed-starting soil mix
Pencil or tweezers
Nail scissors
Watering can with very fine nose
Tray to catch water
Sunny window or plant lights

• Save used cell packs. Sterilize with a weak solution of one part bleach to nine parts water; use them to start your own seeds indoors.
• Place young seedlings in dappled shade before planting. Seedlings transplanted directly from your house to the garden will be shocked.

A Step-by-Step Method

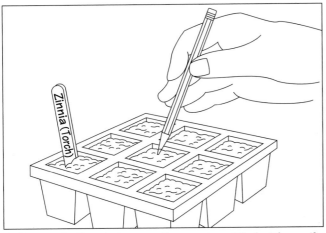

1. Sow seeds directly in a sterile container filled with a soil mix specially formulated for starting seeds. Water the flat before sowing. For fine seeds, use tweezers or the moistened tip of a pencil to place seeds in the containers. Do not bury the seeds, but press them firmly into the mix.

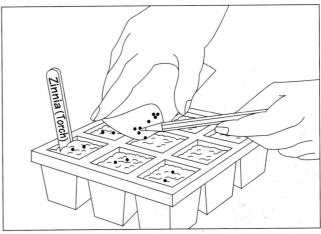

2. Sow two seeds in each cell for insurance. Label each pack with the name and selection of the plant and the planting date. Flat wooden sticks and a fine-tip permanent marker work well.

3. Keep the flat watered with the fine spray of a watering can. To conserve moisture, place the flat in a clear plastic bag, but remove it when the seedlings appear. Do not use a bag if the flat is on a warm surface, such as a water heater.

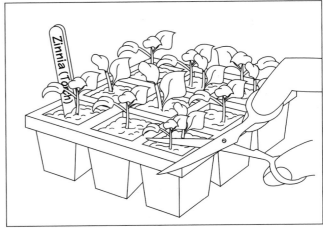

4. In all likelihood, more than one seed will germinate. When this occurs, snip off the smaller seedling at soil level with nail scissors.

Basics of Care

Keep weeds down by using an organic mulch such as pine straw. It also adds organic matter to the soil as it decomposes.

To ensure the success of your flowers, give them basic care after they are planted.

Once you have prepared the soil and gotten your plants in the ground, taking care of your outdoor flowers requires only basic maintenance. Whether planted in the garden or in a pot, flowers need water and food to supply energy and mulch to keep their roots cool and moist. Give flowers these comforts and a bit of individual attention, and they will reward you with colorful blooms.

Caring for Flowers in the Garden

Maintaining your garden is easy when you follow a few basic but essential steps. Learn how much and how often you need to water, mulch, fertilize, and groom your plants. Find out if the perennials in your garden need to be divided. Once you understand your plants' needs, you can keep your flowerbeds beautiful with little effort.

Watering

All flowers need more frequent watering when first planted. Later on, established plants require less water, especially the hardier species. Many methods of watering work: use a sprinkler or a soaker hose, or

A variety of equipment makes getting water to your plants convenient.

simply hold your garden hose over the plants. The key is to water thoroughly to encourage deep rooting. Shallow watering keeps roots close to the surface, making plants more susceptible to drought.

Generally, 1 inch of water per application gets water deep enough in most soil types. Measure this inch by placing sev-

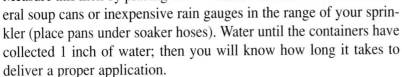

eral soup cans or inexpensive rain gauges in the range of your sprinkler (place pans under soaker hoses). Water until the containers have collected 1 inch of water; then you will know how long it takes to deliver a proper application.

Do not apply the inch of water all at once if your bed is sloped or if the soil drains poorly. Instead, apply until the water becomes puddled or runs off. Turn the sprinkler off for an hour or so to let the water soak in, and then reapply. Remember that sandy soils do not hold water well and dry out faster than clay or rich organic soil.

You do not have to stand watch or come home early just to turn off your sprinkler. Install an automatic irrigation system or an inexpensive timer at the spigot. The economical timers range from mechanical types that simply turn off the water after a set number of minutes (like a kitchen timer) to computerized types that program several days at a time (ideal when you are away on vacation).

Another way to make watering easier is to lay a soaker hose in the bed before setting out your transplants. Made of a porous material, a soaker hose allows water to seep out along its length. If the bed is longer than 20 feet, choose a hose less than ⅝ inch in diameter to ensure better pressure and thus a better flow of water along the entire length of the soaker hose. You can quickly hook and unhook your garden hose to the soaker using snap-type couplers.

FLOWERS THAT ENDURE

These flowers bounce back if they go a week or more without being watered, even during hot, dry weather.

Black-eyed Susan
Boltonia
Butterfly weed
Coreopsis
Gaura
Globe amaranth
Goldenrod
Heliopsis
Klondyke cosmos
Madagascar periwinkle
Moss rose
Purslane
Sedum
Spider flower

Showy sedum blooms in spite of forgotten waterings.

Shredded leaves are an excellent mulch and soil conditioner.

Mulching

Mulch covers the ground like a blanket to help deter the growth of weeds and to keep the soil moist. Organic mulches, such as bark, compost, and shredded leaves, build the richness of soil as they decompose. Mulch also protects plants from temperature extremes. In summer, it keeps the soil around the roots cooler; in winter, it helps prevent alternate freezing and thawing. Half-hardy perennials, such as azure sage, may extend their range a bit farther north when covered with a layer of mulch.

Pine straw, bark nuggets, finely ground bark, and shredded leaves are a few of the many mulches you can use. Choose mulch based on the terrain of your garden or on your personal preference for the color and texture of a particular mulch. Once you have chosen it, apply the mulch 2 to 4 inches thick.

Pine straw clings to gentle slopes better than other mulches because the needles knit together. The easiest way to mulch with pine straw is to apply it *before* planting small transplants. Work and rake the soil smooth for planting; then spread the mulch over the area. As you set out transplants, push a bit of the pine straw aside to clear a spot for each plant; this is easier than trying to knit the long needles together around and between plants after they are in the ground.

If you use bark, compost, or other material that is easily spread, set transplants first and spread the mulch by hand or shovel between the plants. When transplants are small, you can cover each with a plastic cup and work quickly without fear of burying a plant. Simply lift the cups when the bed is mulched.

You can obtain pine straw, one of the best mulching materials, simply by raking fallen pine needles in late summer.

Fertilizing

One look at the fertilizer shelf at the local garden center just might make you want to turn and run. With so many brands and formulas available, you may feel a degree in chemistry would come in handy. However, if you arm yourself with a knowledge of what your plants need, you can feed your garden with minimal fuss.

The purpose of fertilization is to meet a plant's nutritional needs; those needs vary with both the age and the species of the plant. For example, a young transplant or seedling generally needs nitrogen early in its life to support rapid growth. Later, as the plant reaches its full size, nitrogen is less important, and you can encourage blooms with a fertilizer high in phosphorus and potassium but lower in nitrogen. A few plants, such as sweet pea, generally do not need fertilizer at all, because they can generate their own nitrogen provided a certain bacteria is present in the soil. However, most of today's hybrid plants, such as improved daylilies, depend upon good fertilization to reach their full potential. Refer to the individual plant profiles (beginning on page 49) to determine the fertilizer needs of a specific plant.

The easiest and most sensible approach to fertilization is to add adequate nutrients to the soil *before* you plant. In most cases, a high-quality, controlled-release fertilizer will suffice. Perform a soil test to discover any deficiencies or excesses that need correcting. Test results should give specific recommendations to solve the problem. (See page 34 for more about soil testing.)

To enrich your soil, always add compost or other organic matter that is rich in the many nutrients a plant needs. Then work a controlled-release fertilizer into the soil before planting to ensure a constant supply of essential elements. If you use a chemical fertilizer, purchase one that contains at least half of its nitrogen in a controlled-release form.

Water young plants with a diluted fertilizer solution the first week or two after planting to give them a boost. Plants absorb this liquid food immediately. You can use an all-purpose mix, such as 20-20-20 or fish emulsion, on transplants.

The fertilizer label. By law, all fertilizers must carry a label stating the percentage of nutrients they contain. The three numbers always represent the percentage of nitrogen (N), phosphorus (P), and potassium (K). If the package is labeled 10-5-8, it contains 10 percent nitrogen, 5 percent phosphorus, and 8 percent potassium. These are the nutrients most required by a plant, so the combination

These colorful daylilies flourish in well-drained soil that has plenty of organic matter.

The easiest way to add fertilizer to a new bed is to work it into the soil before planting.

WHAT IS A CONTROLLED-RELEASE FERTILIZER?

Controlled-release fertilizer is sometimes called *timed-release* because it releases small amounts of nutrients at a time. The nutrients are coated and held in reserve to be released gradually over several weeks or months, depending on soil moisture and temperature. This type of fertilizer is ideal for the busy gardener because it does not have to be applied often.

The label indicates whether the fertilizer contains controlled-release nitrogen. There is a wide price range depending on the percentage of coated nutrients a fertilizer contains. Look for one that has at least 50 percent controlled-release nitrogen.

of nitrogen, phosphorus, and potassium makes up what is called a complete fertilizer.

Nitrogen stimulates new growth, especially early foliage, which is why plants need a good supply early in the growth cycle. Because nitrogen is very soluble and mobile in the soil, buy a product that contains a controlled-release form. Otherwise, the nitrogen may wash away before being absorbed.

Phosphorus encourages flowering and is essential for overall plant health. Bloom-boosting fertilizers contain a high percentage of phosphorus. However, too much phosphorus in the soil blocks a plant's ability to absorb other nutrients. Unless you are gardening in containers or your soil test indicates a deficiency, use a fertilizer low in phosphorus. Many suburban soils may already be high in phosphorus if the land was once agricultural.

Potassium, also called potash on fertilizer labels, is essential to plant metabolism. It is crucial to a plant's cell wall structure as well as its ability to manufacture food. However, be sure not to use potassium in excess, or it may burn your plants.

Organic fertilizers. Organic gardeners can achieve similar results with natural fertilizers, such as blood meal or organic flower food, which depend upon soil bacteria to release their nitrogen as they decompose. These fertilizers yield good results and may increase microbial activity. Generally, organic fertilizers contain less nitrogen than their chemical counterparts. For example, blood meal is one of the highest in nitrogen, containing between 10 and 12 percent. Cottonseed meal contains about 6 percent nitrogen; composted chicken manure contains only 4 percent. If you compare cost per pound and quantity of nitrogen, these tend to be more expensive than chemical fertilizers.

To help your plants grow to their optimum size, feed them with a quality controlled-release fertilizer.

Grooming

Tall flowers are always an asset to a garden; they create vertical interest and provide depth to a planting. However, they will most likely need the support of a stake or grow-through wire mesh to keep them from falling over. The best time to set the support is when the plant is small so that you do not risk breaking roots or stems by driving in a stake. Begin tying up tall plants when they are about 2 feet tall, and attach them at 1-foot intervals as they grow.

Certain plants bloom longer if you remove the spent flowers before they can form seed. This is called ***deadheading.*** Most annuals respond well to this, as do perennials such as asters, butterfly weed, coreopsis, mums, reblooming daylilies, and salvia. Some perennials, such as astilbe, bluestar, peonies, and most iris, bloom only once a year whether deadheaded or not.

A few perennials also need cutting back during the season to help them keep a neat form. For example, lamb's ears stretches and loses its matlike habit when the blooms appear; snip off the blooms to keep this from happening. Chrysanthemums are another example. They may grow too tall and leggy when left alone, but if trimmed back once or twice in spring and early summer, the plants are fuller and neater and produce more blooms.

Pinch the dead blossoms off petunias, and the plants will flourish.

Snip the blooms off lamb's ears when they appear to help the plant retain its matlike character.

Propagating Perennials

Starting new plants is inherent to growing perennials, as many plants require digging and dividing to rejuvenate the planting. This makes perennials great for sharing.

Dividing. Perennials live a long time and often form clumps or spread. This makes it easy—and economical—to start new plants from existing perennials, to expand a planting, and to give plants away. In fact, most perennials bloom best if they are divided every three or four years, as this encourages vigorous new shoots.

Shasta daisies spread by forming clumps that are easily lifted from the ground with a fork.

Some perennials, such as hosta, have dense roots. You may need the help of a knife or a hatchet to divide clumps of them.

Perennials generally grow larger by sending out new shoots that arise from the base of the original. Arum, blue phlox, daisies, daylilies, hostas, mums, and many others grow this way, eventually forming a clump of multiple shoots or plantlets. To divide, simply dig the clump to separate the pieces. If the crown is dense and the roots are thick and tangled, the plants are not easy to separate. You will need a knife or a hatchet to cut through the tangled mass. As long as the plantlets you have divided still have their healthy shoots and roots intact, this will do them no harm.

After dividing, replant the smaller divisions or place them in pots to give away. Then rejuvenate the bed by adding organic matter to the soil before replanting.

Layering. Some perennials have stems that root where their nodes, or joints, touch the ground. Bath's Pink dianthus and moss verbena are two examples. Often these plants root on their own as the stems creep. To encourage this, dig a small trench, lay a portion of the branch in the trench, and cover it with soil. Put a small rock over a node to ensure that it stays in firm contact with the soil **(Diagram 1).** Later, dig the newly rooted stem, cutting it away from the parent stem **(Diagram 2),** and replant it elsewhere in the garden or in a pot.

Diagram 1

Diagram 2

Caring for Flowers in Containers

Potted plants need more care than plants in the ground because their roots grow within the confines of a pot. They depend on you for soil, fertilizer, and water. However, the color they bring to patios and windows is worth the extra effort.

Selecting Soil

Good soil is crucial to plants in containers. It must drain well and be free of soilborne diseases and insects. Buy premium-quality, sterile potting soil rather than use soil from the yard to fill a pot. Potting soil is a packaged soil mix made especially for growing plants in pots; blend it with composted bark, sphagnum peat moss, sand, perlite, or vermiculite. Some potting soils even contain starter fertilizer. Look for one that lists these quality ingredients.

Manufacturers of potting soil and bagged topsoil are not always required to state the contents of their soil mix, so you will find a big difference in quality among brands. A poor soil can be too acid or too alkaline, may be prone to compaction, or may contain certain ingredients toxic to the plants. Price is generally a good indicator of quality. Do not use leftover seed-starting mix for potting plants; it is so lightweight that it does not anchor large plants well.

Planting in Containers

To plant in a container, cover the drainage hole with a piece of window screen or fine mesh. This lets excess water drain while keeping soil from leaking out. Fill the pot with sterile potting soil to within 1 inch of the rim. (If too full, the soil will wash out when you water.) Space transplants at half the spacing that you would use if planting them in the garden. If you start from seed, sow at the depth recommended on the packet; when the seedlings emerge, thin to about half the recommended spacing.

A POTTING SOIL RECIPE

If you have several pots to fill, it is cheaper to mix your own potting soil. Here is a recipe for a good general mix.

Use a 3-gallon bucket to fill a 3-cubic-foot wheelbarrow with the following:

1 bucket sphagnum peat moss
1 bucket coarse sand
1 bucket finely ground bark
2 cups lime
⅓ pound iron sulfate
2 pounds controlled-release flower food or 6 pounds cottonseed meal

Use your shovel to blend the ingredients. Stir well to be sure the soil is mixed evenly. Gently dampen the mix with a sprinkler, stopping every few minutes to turn the soil thoroughly. When the mix is moist (not soggy), it is ready to use. Store any leftover soil in a large plastic garbage can with a sealed lid.

Fill pots to within 1 inch of the rim with a premium potting soil.

Set transplants in a pot at half the spacing recommended for the garden.

The organic matter in potting soil decomposes with time, so refill your pots with fresh soil every other year. In Florida or other warm, humid climates where decomposition occurs very quickly, you need to refill with fresh soil every year. Recycle old soil by mixing it into your flowerbeds or compost pile.

Fertilizing

Unless a potting soil specifically states that it contains fertilizer, it is probably very low in the elements plants need for growth. When planting, incorporate a controlled-release fertilizer that also contains micronutrients into the mix. Plants require frequent watering during the heat of the summer, which often cuts the life of the fertilizer by one-third to one-half. Be prepared to reapply fertilizer during the growing season.

When filling pots, be sure to include a quality controlled-release fertilizer to provide the nutrients the plants need for growth.

Watering

Plants in containers dry out more quickly than those in the garden. Their small volume of soil does not hold much water, and their exposure to air and heat through the pot causes rapid evaporation. To make watering convenient, keep a hose and watering can nearby. Afternoon shade also reduces heat and stress on plants in midsummer.

In winter, it is easy to forget waterings because plants do not wilt as readily. However, if pansies or other winter flowers are dry when an Arctic blast comes along, they are much more likely to be damaged by the cold. You can spray them with an *antidesiccant* (an agent that prevents visible wilting) to keep their foliage from drying, but do not forget to water them.

FLOWERS THAT THRIVE IN CONTAINERS

Although you can grow just about anything in a container if you give it enough care, the ideal plants require minimal maintenance. They are forgiving (should you forget to water) and stay low enough not to flop over or require staking. The following flowers do very well in pots. Those marked with an asterisk (*) have stems long enough for hanging baskets or for spilling over the edge of a planter.

Ageratum
Artemisia
Dianthus
Dusty miller
Evergreen candytuft*
Geranium
Globe amaranth (dwarf types)
Hosta
Johnny-jump-up
Lisianthus (dwarf types)
Madagascar periwinkle*
Marigold
Melampodium
Moss rose*
Narrow-leaf zinnia*
Ornamental cabbage and kale
Pansy
Petunia*
Rose verbena*
Sedum
Sweet alyssum*
Trailing lantana*
Wax begonia

Petunias and rose verbena are two of an endless number of combinations that thrive in containers.

Annual Profiles

The annuals described in the following pages were selected by the garden editors at *Southern Living* on the basis of their popularity with gardeners throughout the South as well as their adaptability to the region. Arranged alphabetically by common name, the Annual Profiles give you a description of each plant, information about planting and care, and suggested ways that you can incorporate its color, height, and form into your garden. In addition, you'll find troubleshooting tips and solutions to make your gardening a pleasure, not a chore.

When a genus contains more than one related species, such as morning glory and moonflower, they are combined as a single entry. However, the description points out the differences in appearance and growing needs of the most popular species.

For a quick overview of the plant, refer to the *At a Glance* box that accompanies every profile. This will give you the major features of the annual, including its botanical name to help you avoid confusion when buying plants.

You will note that no growing range is given for the annuals. These flowers can generally grow in any Zone, but the time of year will vary. In fact, many of the plants described as an annual may take on traits of a perennial in the warmer climates of the Coastal and Lower South. Experiment with new annuals in your garden each year, and try planting those that you have never grown before or that are only marginally suited to your climate. You may find that even the most unexpected selections will flourish with your tender care; if not, you can begin again with a clean slate next year!

Caladiums

Zinnias

49

Ageratum

The fine-petaled flowers are borne in clusters.

It is so rare to find a flower with blue blooms that gardeners feel they have a treasure in ageratum. Although ageratum comes in an assortment of hues, blue ageratum is prized for its unusual color. Ageratum is also one of the garden's longest lasting blues.

The clusters of ageratum create a dense blanket of flowers that is excellent for edging, planting in masses, or adding a bit of strong color to containers. The dwarf types stay compact, never sprawling or straying, and thus are well suited for a design that requires perfect edges or uniform height.

This plant was very popular during the Victorian era, when carpet bedding (large garden designs made with flowers) was popular. The same use applies today for parterre gardens, or for elaborate garden clocks and other designs painted with flowers across the landscape. Dwarf ageratum also does well in strawberry jars because the compact plants do not outgrow the "pockets" of the planter. Taller selections, although less common, are superb cut flowers. They are better suited for informal cottage gardens or as filler in flower borders.

Ageratum is a good choice for containers. Here it is combined with shrimp plant, gerbera daisy, and narrow-leaf zinnia.

Photographers have noted a phenomenon that is specific to this plant and is often called the "ageratum effect." The blooms of ageratum do not appear blue in photographs. Even the bluest selections appear to be pinkish purple.

Planting and Care

Ageratum does not like hot, dry places. Make every effort to plant it in soil that is rich in organic matter and stays evenly moist, or consider planting something else. When planted in good soil and given fertilizer and regular watering, ageratum produces flowers nonstop from spring until the first fall frost. The blossoms are tiny, fluffy, and closely bunched and by the end of the season may completely blanket the foliage.

While full sun yields the best show, afternoon shade will protect the thin-petaled blooms from scorching in the summer. The hairy, heart-shaped leaves are sensitive to cold and will blacken with the first frost—your signal to replace them with pansies or other cool-weather annuals if you have not already done so.

Ageratum has a vigorous, fibrous root system, and plants will often be root bound when you buy them. Turn to page 30 to read about dealing with root-bound transplants. Set out transplants about two weeks after the last frost.

Different Selections

Blue is by far the most popular color of ageratum, and it comes in a great many shades—sky blue, lavender, and violet blue. Ageratum can also be found in white and shades of pink and burgundy. Dwarf types, such as Blue Danube, Fine Wine, and True Blue, generally grow from 6 to 10 inches tall and spread 12 inches or more. Tall selections, such as Blue Horizon, grow about 24 inches tall and nearly as wide with long, sturdy stems that are perfect for cutting. They are also popular for drying and will hold their color; hang the cut stems upside down to dry.

Fall leaves contrast with ageratum's green, heart-shaped foliage and clusters of flowers.

Troubleshooting

Whiteflies, which are a common greenhouse pest, love this plant, so be sure the plants you bring home from the garden center are not infested. Even if the plants are clean, watch for whiteflies to appear in the garden in late spring and summer. See page 236 to read more about whiteflies.

Black-eyed Susan

Black-eyed Susan provides a familiar and friendly splash of color from mid- to late summer.

Black-eyed Susan is a gardener's delight; it is easy to grow, mixes well with other plants, and is a colorful addition to any setting. The blooms are 2 to 3 inches across and appear atop 3-foot stems from July until mid-September. Each bright yellow flower has a black cone or "eye" in its center, which gives the plant its name.

You can plant black-eyed Susan just about anywhere—in flowerbeds, among shrubs or ground cover, or in a cutting garden. Plant a grouping at the edge of a wood for a natural look. Because of its penetrating color, black-eyed Susan usually looks best when planted in groups, rather than scattered here and there.

As half-hardy perennials, black-eyed Susans may come back year after year, but this is unlikely. Instead, they usually grow leaves the first year and flower the second, much like biennials. They drop seed at the end of the season. You can often see black-eyed Susans colonizing fields and roadsides as a result of their prolific seeding.

Planting and Care

Black-eyed Susan grows best in moist, fertile soil, but the plants also tolerate poor, dry conditions. However, the soil must be well drained; in soggy soil, the roots rot. Full sun produces bushier plants and more blooms, but flowers also appear in light shade.

Sow seed directly in the garden in early spring, or start transplants indoors about six weeks before the last frost. Pat the seed into the soil so that it is in firm contact but not buried in the ground. When the seedlings sprout, thin to about 2 feet apart.

Black-eyed Susan often reseeds itself, so watch for seedlings. The young plants appear as a crown of fuzzy leaves that are similar to those of the parent plant. Dig and transplant seedlings in the spring.

This black-eyed Susan has narrow petals and a small eye, giving it a dainty look.

AT A GLANCE

❖

BLACK-EYED SUSAN
Rudbeckia hirta

Features: vivid yellow blooms from mid- to late summer

Colors: bright yellow

Height: 2 to 3 feet

Light: full sun or light shade

Soil: well drained, fertile to poor

Water: low; wilts, but comes back from drought

Pests: none specific

Remarks: reseeds easily

IS IT ANNUAL OR PERENNIAL?

Perhaps the trickiest thing about black-eyed Susan is matching the name to the correct plant. A related species, *Rudbeckia fulgida*, is often erroneously called black-eyed Susan, but the correct name is orange coneflower. Orange coneflower is fully perennial and does not reseed; it spreads by stems that grow from the base of the plant and creep along the ground to form large masses of plants. Goldsturm is one of orange coneflower's most long-lived and popular selections. (See pages 171 and 172 for more information.)

Gloriosa daisy, a selection of black-eyed Susan, is prized for arrangements because of its artful markings.

Different Selections

The flowers of all black-eyed Susans last for a long time, which makes them excellent cut flowers. Seed catalogs often list a strain of black-eyed Susan called gloriosa daisy. This plant has huge, bicolored blooms that are up to 7 inches across, with mahogany tones streaking toward the center. One selection of gloriosa daisy is called Pinwheel because of this unusual marking. The gloriosa daisy is especially valued for the impact its markings add to an arrangement of cut flowers, as is Irish Eyes, a selection noted for its green center.

Troubleshooting

Although not bothered by insects or diseases, plants may be knocked down by heavy rains. Be prepared to stake them by simply tying their stems to a 3- or 4-foot tomato stake.

Irish Eyes is an unusual selection with a green center.

Cabbage and Kale

Kale has frilly leaves that provide texture and color from fall until spring in areas with mild winters.

AT A GLANCE

❖

CABBAGE AND KALE

Brassica oleracea
var. *acephala*

Features: leafy, bright rosettes, excellent for borders

Colors: green with white to red centers

Height: 6 to 10 inches

Light: full sun

Soil: well drained, fertile

Water: low to medium

Pests: cabbageworms

Remarks: good color and texture in fall and winter

Hardy, colorful versions of culinary cabbage and kale, ornamental cabbage and kale look like giant winter flowers. Their red, lavender, or white centers get brighter after the first frost. These cool-weather annuals thrive when temperatures drop, though they do not tolerate extreme cold. Gardeners in areas with mild winters should plant them in fall and winter for best color.

Use ornamental cabbage and kale in flowerbeds, pots, or even arrangements. Because they are large plants, cabbage and kale can be appreciated from a distance. Planted close together, they are a solid mass of color; placed in a curve around a mix of flowers, they become a handsome border.

Plant them with other cool-weather annuals, such as pansies and sweet William. The darkest shades are a great foil for blue, white, or yellow blooms. For a bold accent, mix these ornamentals singly with plants that have finely textured foliage, such as parsley. Plant them in masses in an unused portion of the vegetable garden to be harvested for tabletop arrangements and garnishes. Although edible, their flavor is inferior to that of culinary cabbage and kale.

Planting and Care

Nurseries may carry ornamental cabbage and kale in various sizes—small transplants, young plants in 4-inch pots, and mature plants in gallon containers. Set plants growing in 4-inch pots or smaller about a foot apart, as they will spread outward as they grow. Large plants, which are instant accents when planted, are not likely to spread after being set in the garden. Place mature plants closer together so that the rosettes almost touch each other.

Plant in full sun for the best color, and keep plants watered during dry weather. Although fairly tolerant of dry soil, young plants will not grow to full size without plenty of water. When given adequate water, sun, and fertilizer, small transplants grow quickly. If the weather turns warm after they are in the ground, cabbage and kale may grow upward from the base and their normally short, hidden stems may grow a bit too long. When this happens, the rosettes seem to be sitting atop tiny "trunks." If this occurs, dig them up and replant deeper, right up to the base of the rosettes, so that their stems are buried.

The bright rosettes of ornamental cabbage and kale should be attractive through the winter unless the temperature regularly dips into the teens. In the spring, you will know that they are ready to be removed when the heads begin to grow tall. If left alone, they stretch to about 2 feet tall and grow a branched stalk of small yellow flowers. Culinary cabbages, collards, and other members of the cabbage family do the same. Some gardeners like the effect, leaving the plant in the garden until the flowers fade.

Different Selections

The leaves of ornamental cabbage and kale may be curly, smooth, or cut around the edges like a fringe. You will find curly-leafed kale and smooth-leafed cabbage in white and purplish pink, all growing about a foot in diameter. Cut-leafed kale, such as Peacock, has a more feathery texture than whole-leafed selections and is easier to knit together in masses. If you live in an area subject to sudden dips into the low teens, choose red-leafed selections; white ones are more likely to turn brown when they freeze.

Cut-leafed selections of kale have a feathery texture.

Starting from Seed

If you wish to grow your own transplants, sow the seed in late summer, about eight weeks before the first frost. It is essential to keep the seedlings cool, but because you will be starting them during hot weather, it can be difficult. Sow them indoors or under lights in a basement. Move young transplants outside when the nights begin to cool in early fall. (See pages 38 and 39 for more about starting seed indoors.)

A full head of cabbage will be almost magenta after a series of frosts.

Troubleshooting

Cabbage and kale are often bothered by cabbageworms—green velvety caterpillars that eat holes in the leaves. Turn to page 234 for more about cabbageworms.

Caladium

The vivid foliage of caladiums is as attractive as the blossoms of other annuals.

Caladiums are among the few annuals grown for their foliage, not their flowers. The large leaves color the summer garden with patterns of white, red, and green, bringing to it a fresh, cool feel. Caladiums thrive in heat but wither quickly in cool weather. However, from midspring until early fall, they are exceptionally easy to grow in shade; some also do well in full sun.

Because of their unique foliage, caladiums are strong visual elements in a garden. They add vivid contrast to a shade garden, brightening those areas not quite sunny enough for most flowering plants. They often grow to 24 inches tall, so you can use them to fill large areas. Try masses of a single selection, or plant two complementary colors under a tree, in an open planting bed, or along a garden path.

Planting and Care

Unlike other annuals, which are generally grown from seed, caladiums sprout from a bulblike tuber. In spring, you will find both transplants in pots and loose tubers for sale. When purchasing tubers, be aware of differences in size. Diameters range from 1 to 3½ inches. The larger the tuber, the fuller the plant will be, so always buy the largest ones available. They cost more, but you will need fewer of them to have a full stand.

Large caladiums punctuate a formal planting of pink and white impatiens.

You can plant caladiums in the spring garden when the soil temperature has reached 70 degrees, usually three to four weeks after the last frost. If planted too early in the season, the tubers may rot.

Plant caladiums in rich, moist, well-drained soil. Place tubers 2 to 3 inches deep and 8 to 18 inches apart (depending on the leaf size of the selection). Place smaller tubers at about half the spacing of large ones; they produce smaller plants and need less room to grow.

Caladiums need a lot of water, especially when planted in full sun. They wilt quickly and go dormant if left too long without water. Mulch the soil around them to help retain moisture. During the summer, *spathes*, or pointed flowering stalks, sprout beneath the leaves; pinch these off when they appear, as flowering discourages the plant from producing more leaves.

Different Selections

There are two basic types of caladiums: fancy leafed and lance leafed. The only real difference between the two is the shape—the fancy leafed is heart shaped, while the lance leafed is arrow shaped. The range of colors and patterns extends from almost pure white Candidum to the burgundies of Irene Dank and Postman Joyner and a host of variegated selections. One of the most popular variegated

An elegant pot with caladiums and asparagus fern is a welcoming accent on this shaded terrace.

This mass planting of white Candidum brings light to a shady bed.

caladiums is Little Miss Muffet, a compact selection (about 10 inches tall) that bears green-and-white leaves with pink specks.

Often caladiums are considered suitable only for areas that have at least partial shade. Candidum Jr., Pink Symphony, and Gypsy Rose have a low tolerance to full sun and do best when planted in a shady location. Yet some do quite well in full sun, especially Aaron, Lance Whorton, Red Frill, and Pink Cloud. Generally, the selections with thick leaves are more tolerant of sun than those with thin leaves.

Save the Tubers

Caladiums are killed by frost. Some gardeners dig up the tubers before the first frost and save them to plant the following spring. To save the tubers, stop watering in early fall and allow the leaves to wither. Once the leaves are yellow and droopy, but before the first frost, dig up the tubers, dust off the soil, snip off the dying leaves, and air-dry in a shaded, well-ventilated area for several days. Pack them in dry sphagnum peat moss, and store indoors at a temperature of about 70 degrees until the next year. You can also store the dry, healthy tubers in a mesh bag hung in a well-ventilated area.

Caladiums blend easily into existing plantings of ferns and hostas, providing additional summer color.

A mix of caladiums and impatiens creates a stunning yet easy-to-grow shady border framed by lush ferns.

Calliopsis

This rugged annual, native throughout most of the United States, is often called plains coreopsis or golden tickseed. It is a 3-foot-tall, upright plant with long, wiry stems and divided leaves. Its yellow pinwheel flowers have vivid maroon centers; the name calliopsis means "beautiful eye." While tough enough to grow on the roadside and in the cracks of sidewalks, it is also graceful, lending a rich golden glow to problem areas of flowerbeds.

Calliopsis is excellent for meadows, street-side plantings, and other hot, hard-to-water places, as well as the lush conditions of a well-prepared flowerbed. It looks superb in large groupings, creating a flowery blanket of color to fill a large area. It mixes nicely with other wildflowers, such as Queen Anne's lace, or with other summer annuals, such as cosmos. The tall stems make ideal cut flowers, staying crisp and pretty in a vase for more than a week.

Planting and Care

Calliopsis thrives on neglect and is often seen growing in highway medians. It is tolerant of every soil type: clay or sandy, acid or alkaline. Drainage is not important to these adaptable plants; they grow in both soggy and dry conditions.

The plant develops a long central root that resents transplanting, so it is best to sow the seed directly in the garden. Thin seedlings to about 8 inches apart. For best flowering, plant in full sun anywhere you would like to see a drift of green, yellow, and maroon. Sow seed in the fall in the South and in spring farther north. Seed sown in the fall produces green rosettes that last through winter. Plants then grow taller in the spring, blooming for four to six weeks in early summer in the South and throughout the summer in cooler regions.

Remove spent flowers to encourage a longer period of bloom. Or try shearing plants back; this often inspires a second round of flowers in early fall. If you want the plants to reseed, however, leave the flowers to produce seeds. Calliopsis reseeds prolifically, and it usually reappears on its own year after year. You can also save your own seeds to replant the next year.

Different Selections

Catalogs list many types of coreopsis; most of these are perennial. However, calliopsis is an annual and still grows in the wild; only a few named selections are available. Dwarf red plains coreopsis is a red plant that grows 1 to 2 feet tall and has solid crimson flowers.

Golden blossoms with mahogany-red centers are the signature of calliopsis, a great flower for seeding a meadow.

AT A GLANCE
❖
CALLIOPSIS
Coreopsis tinctoria

Features: heat-tolerant native with bright summer flowers

Colors: golden yellow with maroon centers

Height: 1 to 3 feet

Light: full sun

Soil: average to poor, acid to alkaline

Water: low to medium

Pests: none specific

Remarks: excellent cut flower

Celosia

The vibrant plumes of this celosia combine with its lime green foliage to add an exotic, tropical look to a summer garden.

Prized for its flamboyance in Victorian gardens, celosia remains popular today among gardeners who recognize its usefulness. Celosia is a reliable source of long-lasting, heat-tolerant color in mid-summer and early fall. The colors of its blooms range from warm pinks and creams to the hot tones of red, purple, and gold, and their unique forms are a delightful novelty.

Celosia ranges from 6 to 36 inches in height, with plume selections serving as a vertical accent in a flowerbed or flower pot. Dwarf selections can be grouped to form a wave of color and texture at the front of a bed or border. Taller celosia can add interest to the back of a border or a rock garden or to the center of an island bed. Plant a large grouping for a dramatic effect, or use small groups, five to seven plants, to draw the eye to a birdbath, a fountain, or a water garden.

Taller selections of plumed celosia are an excellent choice for the center of a flowerbed.

AT A GLANCE

❖

CELOSIA
Celosia cristata

Features: colorful, feathery plumes or crested blooms

Colors: yellow, white, orange, red, purple, light pink

Height: 6 to 36 inches

Light: full sun or partial shade

Soil: moist, fertile

Water: medium to high

Pests: powdery mildew

Remarks: ideal for dried flower arrangements

Different Selections

One type of celosia, Plumosa, is topped with an exotic plume that looks like a cluster of feathers. The Castle series, which stands 12 to 14 inches tall, has clusters of scarlet, yellow, or pink plumes. Apricot Brandy, a soft orange All-America Selections winner, grows to 16 inches tall. Plumed celosia is ideal as a background flower for low-growing bedding plants, such as ageratum or marigolds. Use a dwarf selection, such as the 6-inch Kimono, along a border.

The blooms of another celosia, Cristata, form a velvety crest. This plant is often called cockscomb because the crest resembles the comb of a rooster. Crested celosia is also used in beds and borders as a curiosity. Red Velvet, which has huge crimson blooms, and Jewel Box, dwarf 4- to 5-inch plants in red or gold, work well as novelties when paired with other annuals.

Mass celosia in front of evergreen shrubs to spotlight its unusual blooms. Pair celosia with other flowers in borders; a tall crimson cockscomb, such as Floradale, looks great behind a mix of pink, purple, and white dwarf globe amaranth. A medium-sized plumed selection, such as Red Glow, marries well with tall cosmos and daisies.

Growers have introduced wheat celosia, a Spicata hybrid, that is covered in small silvery pink and purple spikes. Because it looks like a wildflower, this is an ideal annual for a naturalistic landscape such as a rock garden. This annual has all the beauty of a wild grass with the bonus of elegant flowers. Selections of wheat celosia include Pink Candle, which bears rose-pink spikes, Flamingo Feather, a soft pink that fades to white, and Flamingo Purple, with purple plumes and dark reddish green leaves. With its 3½-foot-tall stems and tapered spikes, wheat celosia is an excellent addition to both the landscape and the cutting garden.

Planting and Care

Hybrids grow best when started from transplants. They are difficult to start from seed because they must be kept uniformly warm and moist. Old-fashioned selections are less finicky and easier to grow from seed in the garden or in flats to be transplanted outdoors. Make sure you do not sow seeds or set out transplants until the soil temperature is warm, about two to three weeks after the last frost.

It is crucial not to set celosia out too early because cool temperatures can stunt its growth. Give transplants plenty of room to branch; pinching the center of plumed blooms encourages the plant to form many smaller "feathers" from side branches. (Do not pinch if you want to grow large plumes for cutting or drying.) Be sure celosia gets plenty of water throughout its early growth. If young hybrids are not watered properly, they will not bloom well once they mature.

Troubleshooting

Plants are occasionally bothered by powdery mildew, which looks like a white powder on the leaves. See page 235 for more about powdery mildew.

This hybrid, wheat celosia, looks like a wildflower and works well in naturalistic plantings.

FLOWERS FOR DRYING

Tall selections of plumed, crested, and wheat celosia are popular when dried for use in arrangements and crafts. Simply cut the flowers and hang them upside down for a week. The blooms last a long time and keep their color; after a year or so, they fade to a pale, antiqued shade.

Coleus

Coleus foliage is as bright as a flower.

Coleus has so many shades of foliage that it is hard to believe the leaves are real. The leaves are every bit as showy as a flower. Coleus is available in reds, greens, copper, and white and provides texture and color in gardens. Best of all, it grows in the shade, where vivid color is rare. Many selections also thrive in direct sun.

Coleus will brighten a wooded area with foliage that lasts until the first frost. One or two plants set among ferns in the shade will bring a nice spot of color to the green. It is also great along the north side of a house, where there is little direct sunlight, or as a filler in perennial beds, where it grows large and bushy and where the color of its leaves never fades.

Planted in a pot or a hanging basket, coleus fills out quickly, making a neat, full plant. If a bed needs a summertime pick-me-up, remove the potted plant from its container and plant it directly in the garden. Water it daily if needed until the roots become established.

AT A GLANCE

COLEUS
Solenostemon scutellarioides

Features: multicolored foliage from spring until frost

Colors: white, yellow, red to pink, copper, dark green to chartreuse, variegated combinations

Height: 6 to 36 inches

Light: full sun to shade

Soil: moist, fertile to poor

Water: medium to high; wilts, but comes back from drought

Pests: none specific

Remarks: color rarely fades

Coleus is excellent for mixing with ferns and other finely textured foliage in shade.

Planting and Care

Coleus will not grow unless the weather is warm. A late frost will kill them, so do not be tempted to set plants out early. If you start with transplants, plant at least two weeks after the last frost. Tall selections can be kept fuller by pinching the tips of the stems every month or so as the plants grow. In late summer, coleus sends up spikes of small blue flowers; pinch the flowers as they appear to keep the plants full.

This large-leafed pink-and-green coleus punctuates a summer flowerbed, bringing a contrast of texture as well as lasting color until frost.

From top: *Sunset Wizard, Golden Dragon*

Coleus does not require extra fertilizer through the season, but it does need plenty of water. Large-leafed selections may droop in summer heat and dry weather, but they recover quickly if watered before they become completely dry.

Different Selections

Perhaps the most perplexing aspect of growing coleus is choosing a selection, as they vary greatly in appearance. Coleus grows from 6 to 36 inches in height, and its leaves may be small and lobed or large and full. Color is also an issue, because coleus comes in a rainbow of shades. The Carefree series are dwarf, bushy plants that you can recognize easily by their small, lobed leaves. These plants grow only 8 to 12 inches tall, so they are excellent for small pots. Wizard is another popular series; these plants grow 1 to 2 feet tall and have heart-shaped leaves.

The leaves of some selections lose their color in full sun, especially in dry climates. If your coleus will be in sun all day, look for selections that have been especially bred to tolerate the sun, such as Alabama Sunset. The Sunlovers series includes selections that grow in full sun; these do not flower in summer, so there is no need to pinch the leaves. Plum Parfait and Burgundy Sun are dark reds that tolerate full sun. Red Ruffles, Cranberry Salad, Freckles, and Rustic Orange grow in both full sun and in the shade.

Starting from Seed

Gardeners sometimes choose to grow coleus from seed if a particular color is not available at local garden centers. You can grow transplants by starting seeds indoors six to eight weeks before the last frost date. The seeds need light to germinate, so gently pat them into the seed-starting mix with your fingertips to be sure that they are not buried. For best germination, keep the soil at 70 degrees or slightly warmer. (See pages 38 and 39 for more about starting seed indoors.)

Red Wizard

Cosmos

This annual's name was derived from the Greek word kosmos, *which means "beautiful thing."*

The soft color of cosmos makes it a delightful transitional annual.

Cosmos can be a gardener's best friend in late summer, when other plants are fading. This carefree annual boasts charming blooms in two dazzling color ranges: lustrous pink, rose, and white; and radiant yellow, orange, and tomato red. It is so easy to grow that you need only sow the seed in a sunny place and watch this fast-growing, sun-loving plant thrive.

Common cosmos, *Cosmos bipinnatus,* offers billowy, fern-like foliage and 4-inch-wide, daisylike flowers. It does well in mass plantings or near the back of a border, where it can grow to 4 to 5 feet in height. Pair it with hollyhocks, fall veronicas, or purple coneflower for comely combinations. Klondyke cosmos, *Cosmos sulphureus,* is sometimes called yellow cosmos or orange cosmos and bears a smaller bloom than *Cosmos bipinnatus.* Dwarf selections of Klondyke cosmos are ideal for the front of a border or bed, or as a container plant, especially when mixed with plants that have more dense foliage, such as English ivy or creeping lantana.

Cosmos is often grown for its dependability as a cut flower. Once you get accustomed to having these informal bouquets in your home, they will become a summer tradition. Another plus for cosmos is that it blooms until the first frost, extending its colorful presence well into the fall garden. Klondyke cosmos attracts bees, butterflies, and, when it sets seed, goldfinches. Klondyke cosmos has sparse foliage, so plant it behind short, dense plants to conceal its leggy stems.

Planting and Care

Both types of cosmos are easy to sow directly in the garden. When sown in spring, cosmos grows in poor to average soil, tolerating heat and humidity, and blooms in just 10 to 12 weeks. Scatter seeds on the ground without burying them. Sow in well-drained soil in full sun after all danger of frost is past. Once plants are established, they will tolerate high temperatures and dry spells. Do not overfertilize or plant in rich soil, or you will get a lot of foliage but few flowers.

AT A GLANCE
❖
COMMON COSMOS
Cosmos bipinnatus

Features: heat-tolerant annual with daisylike flowers

Colors: white, pink, lavender, rose, crimson

Height: 2 to 5 feet

Light: full sun

Soil: well drained, poor to fertile

Water: low

Pests: none specific

Remarks: dependable color, grown as a cut flower

Cosmos has thin stems that often require staking. You should pinch plants early in the season to encourage growth. To keep both types of cosmos blooming, cut flowers back as they fade, if you are not cutting them to bring indoors. Klondyke cosmos blooms on long, wiry stems; you can cut the plants back to a foot high in midsummer to encourage a fresh flush of flowers.

On a sunny day, the blossoms of Klondyke cosmos have a near-fluorescent glow.

Different Selections

Common cosmos features the award-winning Sonata series, which are compact, grow to 2 feet tall, and bloom in white or a mix of white, pink, and rose with charming yellow eyes. Sensation Mixed is another favorite, with crimson, pink, and white blooms on wispy 4-foot-tall stems.

Klondyke selections include the Lady Bird series, which are compact, early-blooming plants that grow to a foot tall and bear semidouble flowers in orange and yellow. Sunny Red is a 2-foot-tall All-America Selections winner with bright scarlet, single flowers that soften to orange as they mature. Bright Lights Mixed bears early, semidouble flowers in a mix of yellow, gold, orange, and scarlet on 3-foot-tall stems. Diablo, another All-America Selections winner, has orange-red flowers on a 1½- to 2-foot plant.

Starting from Seed

You can also grow your own transplants about five to seven weeks before the last frost. Because the plants reseed so easily, you can encourage a second crop in the same year by letting some of the first flowers that appear produce seed. Seeds that drop to the ground will germinate and grow quickly in warm summer weather.

AT A GLANCE
❖
KLONDYKE COSMOS
Cosmos sulphureus

Features: upright annual with neon-bright flowers

Colors: yellow, gold, orange, crimson

Height: 1 to 3 feet

Light: full sun

Soil: well drained, poor to average

Water: low

Pests: none specific

Remarks: great cut flower, attracts butterflies and goldfinches

Pinwheels of color brighten a midsummer garden as the wiry stems of Klondyke cosmos billow out from a wooden fence.

Dusty Miller

Dusty miller's silvery hue glows in moonlight.

The frosty foliage of dusty miller seems to have been created simply to make other plants look good. The silvery hue of this modest plant enhances the plants around it, intensifying the colors of adjacent blossoms and the green of nearby leaves. It brings soft, cool color and fine, feathery texture to beds, borders, and containers.

For a pleasing contrast, plant dusty miller against a backdrop of brightly colored annuals, such as yellow marigolds. For a softer effect, pair it with pink, purple, or blue blooms, such as sweet William, petunia, or globe amaranth. Or plant it at the front of a perennial bed at the base of an evergreen border. To separate brightly colored flowers in a bed, plant dusty miller as a transition between different hues, neutralizing the contrast. Compact selections are great for edging an herb garden or brightening rock gardens and containers, where they mix well with just about any flower.

Dusty miller foliage shows up well under moonlight and other night lighting, which makes it a good companion for plantings near decks, patios, and walkways. Its woolly texture also adds to its appeal, as children like to touch the fuzzy leaves.

Dusty miller makes an excellent edging for an evergreen border, with its gray-green foliage bringing out the richness of surrounding colors.

AT A GLANCE
❖
DUSTY MILLER
Senecio cineraria

Features: woolly, old-fashioned plant prized for its foliage
Colors: silver, gray green
Height: 6 to 12 inches
Light: full sun to very light shade
Soil: well drained
Water: low
Pests: none specific
Remarks: very drought tolerant

Planting and Care

Dusty miller is a perennial in the Lower South but may be treated as an annual farther north. Start it from seeds or transplants; it will tolerate freezing weather, so go ahead and plant up to two months before the first fall frost. Choose a sunny area of well-drained, slightly sandy soil. If you sow seed directly in the garden, do not cover; dusty miller needs light to germinate.

Dusty miller is drought tolerant, but keep new plants watered until they are well established. Remove the yellow flowers that appear in May and June to keep foliage looking its best until fall. Midway through the season, dusty miller may get leggy; if so, cut the plants back to about half their height to encourage branching and more compact growth. In areas where it is perennial, cut it back to the ground in late winter before new growth begins.

Different Selections

Silver Queen makes a nice choice for garden borders, growing only 8 inches tall. Another option is Silver Dust, which reaches 9 to 12 inches in height and bears fine, lacy foliage. Cirrus is a compact plant with lobed leaves that grows from 6 to 8 inches tall. Silver Lace is really a different species, *Chrysanthemum ptarmiciflorum*, that may be labeled as dusty miller. It has very fine, lacy foliage and grows 24 inches tall, making a nice addition to a large container.

Both drought and sun tolerant, dusty miller finds a perfect summer home in containers, where it is forgiving when you forget to water.

Four O'Clock

The trumpetlike four o'clock is easy to grow.

This annual is covered with trumpet-shaped blooms that open in late afternoon—around four o'clock—from midsummer until the first frost. The plants are a fragrant addition to the summer garden and are especially nice for gardeners who are away from home until late afternoon each day. Known for centuries as the Marvel of Peru, old-fashioned four o'clock continues to amaze gardeners with its reliable ability to "tell time" and perfume the air as the sun wanes.

Four o'clocks have heavy, multibranched stems and medium-sized leaves. Colorful and easy to grow, this fast-growing annual will develop into a small shrub by midsummer. Use four o'clocks anywhere you need to fill a gap with a 2- to 3-foot-tall flowering shrub, such as near a new foundation, in a sunny, mixed border, at steps leading to a deck or porch, or along a fence or other structure. It also makes an excellent low hedge or screen for an informal cottage garden. Use it to fill any bare space where you can enjoy its nighttime bouquet. Children will enjoy watching four o'clocks open and release their lemony, sweet scent, a dependable part of every afternoon.

Planting and Care

A tender perennial in the Lower and Coastal South and warmer portions of the Middle South, four o'clock is more frequently grown as a hardy annual. It returns each summer from seed without any encouragement on your part.

New plants are easy to start from seed, but the seeds are tough. Soak seeds for a few hours before planting to allow seedlings to break through more easily. After all threat of frost is past, sow seeds about ¼ inch deep in full sun or light shade in well-drained soil. Or start seeds indoors four to six weeks before the last frost.

If you have a friend or neighbor with four o'clocks, you can dig up and divide the tubers in the fall, store them in a cool, dry place during the winter, and plant them in the spring. Set out tubers or transplants 2 feet apart. In warmer regions of the South, the tubers are winter-hardy, and plants are perennial. After the second year, the

---

AT A GLANCE
❖

FOUR O'CLOCK
Mirabilis jalapa

Features: old-fashioned annual covered with fragrant, tubular blooms

Colors: red, pink, yellow, violet, multicolored

Height: 2 to 3 feet

Light: full sun to light shade

Soil: well drained

Water: medium

Pests: Japanese beetles

Remarks: self-sows, perfumes the night air

plants spread by tubers, popping up several inches away from the original. Seedlings may also sprout nearby. Farther north, the only way to have four o'clocks year after year is to save the tubers or let the flowers reseed.

Different Selections

Many gardeners do not know what selection they have in their gardens because they got their seed from a friend or it appeared naturally. Jingles is a named selection with bicolored flowers. Often seeds are just sold as Mixed, meaning a variety of colors—usually pink, yellow, orange, white, and red— are contained in the packet.

Troubleshooting

Four o'clocks may be bothered by Japanese beetles. Turn to page 235 for more about this pest.

A floral timepiece, four o'clock opens every afternoon just before suppertime with a colorful mix of blooms.

Foxglove

For an elegant touch, plant shorter selections in an urn or other large container placed beside your home's entry or on a terrace.

Few plants rival the spires of foxglove for adding stately drama to a bed or border. Easy to grow from transplants, foxgloves are a pleasure not to be missed, whether you enjoy their colorful embroidery from a distance or the charm of their freckled blossoms up close.

Foxgloves boast large, bell-shaped blooms in colors ranging from white, yellow, and shell pink to lavender, magenta, and deep rose. Plant them wherever you need a tall bloom and want to draw attention. They can be spectacular in a border, in a showy corner, around the mailbox, and even in a container.

Planting and Care

Foxgloves enjoy partial shade and moist, well-drained soil. If you have sand or hard clay, add plenty of organic matter before you plant. Space plants 1 to 1½ feet apart to allow room for the foliage to expand.

Foxgloves are biennial, growing leaves one year and blooming the next. Look for plants in quart containers (or larger) with six or more large leaves to set out in fall for blooms the following spring. In most of the South, transplants set out in the fall remain a handsome rosette of foliage through winter. Farther north or during hard winters, freezes may knock back the foliage but will not hurt the roots.

In the spring, the flower stalk rockets skyward until it stands 2 to 7 feet tall, depending upon the selection. It is best to enjoy

In spring, foxgloves stand tall with exquisite bold spires, drawing attention to themselves and giving a strong vertical accent to a flower garden.

foxgloves from late April through June; then after the plants flower, replace them with summer annuals.

You may find mature plants for sale at garden centers in late winter or early spring; these may bloom the first year, depending on their size and how early you set them out. If not, they will certainly bloom the next spring.

Different Selections

Whether you buy plants locally or order seed through the mail, you will find several selections. Excelsior Hybrids are probably the most popular, growing in a mixture of white, pink, and purple. Although the stalks are quite strong, the plants grow 5 to 7 feet tall and can get heavy when the flowers are fully open. Be prepared to stake these taller selections to keep spring storms from destroying a beautiful display.

Foxy Mixed is an All-America Selections winner that blooms quickly, often in the first season if planted in fall in the South or in spring in the North. It is smaller than the more popular foxgloves, with a single majestic spike that is supposed to grow only 3 feet high but generally exceeds that height in the South. Tall foxgloves will produce many smaller spikes if snipped back in the spring when the rosette begins to sprout a stalk.

Cutting

Foxgloves make fine additions to a spring bouquet of cut flowers. Cutting is also a good way to control exceptionally tall plants. By the time the tip of the stalk begins to bloom, the lower portions are producing ripening seeds. If you cut off the stalk at this point, the plant usually sprouts more spikes, although they are never as big or as showy as the first ones. If you leave the seeds, the plants may self-sow, reseeding themselves so that they produce new seedlings each year.

Troubleshooting

In the summer, foxgloves may become weak and bedraggled when spider mites attack the foliage. Rather than spraying, it is easier to pull up the plants each spring, replace them with summer annuals, and then plant strong, new foxgloves in fall. Turn to page 236 to read more about spider mites.

A foreground of pansies is perfect for shorter selections of foxglove.

Geranium

Three pots filled with red geraniums accent the steps of this terrace.

No matter where they grow, geraniums are easily recognized from a distance. Their brightly colored blooms grow in clusters on long stems that stand above abundant foliage. Though they will grow when planted in the garden, geraniums are especially suited to containers. Almost like a pedestal, a pot elevates the blooms, increasing the impact of their showy clusters. Make the most of these vivid blooms by using geraniums to accent an entry, pinpoint a fountain or other garden feature, grace a table, or fill a window box.

Planting and Care

Most geraniums can be started only from cuttings and transplants. Those grown from seed (often called seed geraniums) are very difficult to start at home. Unless you have a greenhouse, begin with purchased transplants. Geraniums need full sun and well-drained, fertile soil that stays moist. Never let the soil in the bed or the container dry, or the leaves will begin to turn yellow; on the other hand, do not let the soil stay soggy, or the roots will rot. When potting geraniums (or any annual) in a container, buy a soil mix that is pH balanced. In a pot or in a flowerbed, raise the pH to about 6.5 by adding lime; most geraniums do not like strongly acid soil.

In the South, geraniums appreciate some shade in the afternoon. However, whether they receive afternoon shade or not, many selections slow down or stop producing blooms until the nights cool down in late August or September. Just keep them watered and fertilized, and you will be pleased by their revival in the fall. To encourage the production of new blooms, remove old flowers as they fade and use a bloom-boosting fertilizer, such as 15-30-15, which contains the proper ratio of nitrogen to phosphorus and potassium.

AT A GLANCE

❖

GERANIUM
Pelargonium x *hortorum*

Features: bright spots of color from early summer to frost

Colors: white, pink, scarlet, salmon, orange, lavender

Height: 12 to 25 inches

Light: full sun, afternoon shade

Soil: well drained, fertile

Water: medium to high

Pests: whiteflies

Remarks: great for mass plantings, pots, window boxes

Different Selections

The most popular geraniums grow from 18 to 25 inches tall and bear attractive, lily pad-shaped foliage. The leaves often vary in hue and may have a dark ring. To avoid a summer pause of blooms in the South, try selections known to be less susceptible to heat. These include the Orbit series, the Pinto series, the Americana series, and Freckles, an All-America Selections winner. These selections are vigorous and have a fuller habit, allowing them to tolerate tough Southern summers.

Dynamo and Elite are compact plants with plentiful blooms. A few geraniums, such as Marilyn, Grace, and Judy, have a habit that is low and spreading and may be used as a seasonal ground cover. They are also good for hanging baskets, window boxes, or hayracks hung on the rails of a deck.

Occasionally you will see geraniums called Floribunda, which refers to the free flowering of many of the types started from seed. Generally they have small, simple blooms rather than giant lollipop-like double blooms. Those with giant double flowers are spectacular, but their petals tend to turn an unsightly brown as the flowers fade.

Ivy-leafed geraniums *(Pelargonium peltatum),* which have trailing stems and ivylike leaves, are the least heat tolerant of geraniums. Although they do well through summer in cooler climates, they struggle in the South. If you buy these in spring for a basket or window box, be prepared to nurse them through a hot summer with plenty of water; they will be dormant through summer but should enjoy a revival in the fall. In Florida and South Texas, they are grown as winter annuals.

Troubleshooting

Whiteflies are a major pest of geraniums. To avoid introducing whiteflies to your garden, be sure to buy plants that are not infested. See page 236 for more about whiteflies.

Some geraniums produce smaller blooms, but they bear more of them than the large-flowered types.

Globe Amaranth

Globe amaranth is valued for its intense color. The papery blossoms are also attractive to skipper butterflies.

Globe amaranth is prized for its ability to produce hundreds of colorful, cloverlike blooms that hardly ever fade, even in mid-summer. Undaunted by heat, each flower glows in shades of purple, pink, white, orange, or red. Globe amaranth is also valued for its use as a dried flower; upon close inspection, the flowers appear to be made of rice paper. When cut at the peak of their color, the papery blooms retain their pigment up to a year, making globe amaranth a popular choice for dried arrangements, wreaths, and other crafts.

Use globe amaranth in flowerbeds, for edgings, or in containers. Dwarf types make excellent choices for pots and window boxes because they are compact and drought tolerant. Any selection will work nicely in front of taller annuals, such as Queen Anne's lace. For brilliant contrast, combine purple globe amaranth with the yellow of black-eyed Susan or the orange of narrow-leaf zinnia. For a softer look, try lavender selections with blue ageratum or silver dusty miller. In addition to being visually attractive, the blooms of globe amaranth attract butterflies.

Planting and Care

You can plant globe amaranth in the spring from transplants or from seed sown directly in the garden. Sow seeds in full sun in well-drained soil. Globe amaranth does not grow well in soggy soil but is tolerant of poor, sandy soil or heavy clay as long as it has adequate drainage.

If you set out transplants, do so in spring after all danger of frost has passed. Water the young plants regularly for the first few weeks; after that, the plants need no attention other than occasional watering during periods of extended drought. Globe amaranth will reseed; look for seedlings to reappear in the garden the next spring.

If you want to dry globe amaranth blossoms, cut the stems before the flowers have fully opened and hang them upside down in a well-ventilated room.

Different Selections

There are many different selections of globe amaranth. Buddy is a short, compact plant (10 to 12 inches tall) with white or purple blooms and is suited for flowerbeds and containers. Dwarf White and Gnome produce neat, petite plants that grow only 8 to 10 inches tall. Taller selections are better for cutting, growing about 2½ feet tall, and include Lavender Lady, Pomponette Pink, and Pomponette

White. Strawberry Fields is a tall, bright red globe amaranth. Tall selections tend to flop over after a hard rain but do not need to be staked—they will stand up on their own.

Starting from Seed

You may need to start your own transplants to assure that you grow the color of blooms you want. Soak the seeds overnight; then sow indoors 8 to 10 weeks before the last frost. Be patient; seeds of globe amaranth are slow to germinate but sprout in two to three weeks in 70 to 75 degree soil. (See pages 38 and 39 for more about starting seed indoors.)

There are many selections of globe amaranth, including this red one, Strawberry Fields.

Purple and pink globe amaranth last from summer through fall. Here they are combined with perennial Autumn Joy sedum.

Hollyhock

Double-flowered hollyhocks add dramatic color to a midsummer garden.

The quintessential English garden flowers, hollyhocks are popular for their romance and nostalgia, as well as their strong vertical presentation. Beginning in early summer, some rise to 8 feet tall, with the upper portions of their stalks loaded with colorful, paperlike blooms measuring 3 to 6 inches across.

Dramatic in both size and shape, hollyhocks will draw attention wherever they are planted. They are stately when added to the back of a border or charming as foundation plantings for a country home. Hollyhocks also work well as colorful screens and are terrific accents for beds or wildflower gardens.

Plant hollyhocks in groups in front of a wall or a weathered fence or against the sunny side of a deck. Hollyhocks are easy to grow and and fun for children, as taller selections will surpass them in height. As an added bonus, your plants may also be visited by hummingbirds.

Planting and Care

Hollyhocks are often labeled perennial but are grown as annuals or biennials in most areas. They are very susceptible to diseases and pests and usually need to be pulled up by the end of the season.

You can start plants from seed or from transplants. Choose a sunny spot with well-drained soil. Sow seeds or set out transplants in the fall in the Coastal, Lower, and Middle South. Farther north, plant in spring when the soil can be easily worked. Hollyhocks thrive in sun and do not mind heat, but the huge blooms and thick leaves need regular watering.

Different Selections

There are many different selections of hollyhock, ranging from 2 to 8 feet tall. Traditional hollyhocks bear single blooms, while newer selections have frilled, double blooms. Powderpuff Mixed features 4-inch-wide red, white, yellow, or pink double blooms on 5-foot-tall shrubby plants. Fordhook Giants Mixed offers masses of colorful double flowers on 6-foot stalks. Character's Double Mixed produces 6- to 8-foot plants that also bear double blooms in an array of colors from white, yellow, and pink to red, maroon, and copper. Alcea Country Garden Mixed brings back old-fashioned single blooms that add charm to informal gardens in a wide range of colors.

Show off the architectural qualities of hollyhocks by placing them in front of a wall or other structure. Here they are accompanied by another old-fashioned favorite, larkspur.

Troubleshooting

Hollyhocks are susceptible to hollyhock rust, a fungal disease that develops on the underside of the leaves and weakens the plant. Allow plenty of spacing between plants for good air circulation as a preventive measure. Hollyhocks can also fall victim to caterpillars, Japanese beetles, and spider mites, especially in hot climates. Be prepared to spray them several times. See pages 234–236 for more about these pests.

Impatiens

Healthy impatiens are covered with blooms from spring until fall.

Blooming nonstop from spring until the first frost, impatiens find their way into more gardens than any other summer annual. Low-maintenance, tropical hybrids, they need only a few hours of sun to produce dazzling mounds of flowers for five to seven months. Impatiens come in more than 15 different colors—from shimmering whites and pale pinks to vivid purples and bright oranges. Faithful bloomers in the shade, impatiens are by far America's best-selling bedding plants.

Use this versatile annual to enliven evergreen shrub borders, or mass it for waves of color. You can also strategically fill holes in shade gardens by setting out a few plants. Or let impatiens colorfully cascade from hanging baskets and containers near an entry, a terrace, or a deck. Impatiens work well as a ground cover in woodland settings, mixed with ferns, caladiums, and other shade lovers for a cool effect.

AT A GLANCE
❖

IMPATIENS
Impatiens wallerana and New Guinea hybrids

Features: nonstop blooms from spring until frost

Colors: white, pink, lavender, orange, red, purple

Height: 6 to 26 inches

Light: shade to partial shade, morning sun

Soil: moist but well drained

Water: high, wilts in afternoon, keep soil evenly moist

Pests: slugs

Remarks: New Guinea impatiens tolerate full sun, all impatiens grow well in partial shade

Planting and Care

The easiest way to start impatiens is to purchase transplants after the last frost. However, in wooded areas, you may choose to scatter the fine seed directly in the garden. Often impatiens reseed themselves, although the offspring will not always look like the original.

Plant impatiens in the shade or in areas that are shaded in the afternoon. Although many selections can tolerate sun, they will need an excessive amount of water during the summer. No matter where they grow, impatiens need a lot of water during dry spells. Be sure to provide adequate moisture, and they will bloom profusely until the fall.

You do not need to pinch blooms to keep impatiens continuously blooming. However, you may need to fertilize them a second time during the season if the leaves turn light green.

When impatiens seedpods are ripe and full, the slightest touch will cause them to burst, scattering seeds to the wind. You can save seeds for the next year by storing them in a dry glass jar. To save a particular plant over winter, take cuttings or move the plant indoors before the first frost. Once the cuttings are rooted, plant them in pots on a sunny windowsill. Remember that the offspring will bear blooms of colors different from the original plants.

A multicolored mix is one of the most popular ways to plant impatiens.

Starting from Seed

It is easier to start impatiens from transplants. If you want to grow them from seed, remember that the seed is very fine, so sow carefully. Use a salt shaker to make the tiny seeds easier to spread over the bed, and be sure to keep the area watered.

Though considered difficult to germinate, the seeds of impatiens sprout quickly if they receive proper care. Sow seed six to eight weeks before the last spring frost. The seeds need light to germinate, so never cover. Instead, pat them gently into contact with the soil. Keep the seeds moist so that they do not dry out; at a temperature between 70 and 75 degrees, seedlings will sprout in about 10 days. Transfer the seedlings to small pots. When they are about 3 inches tall, you can set them in the garden, about 18 inches apart. (Turn to pages 38 and 39 for more about starting seed indoors.)

Most New Guinea impatiens do not grow well from seed. Selections that can be grown from seed include Tango and Spectra.

In shady spots, impatiens bloom profusely, complementing neighboring ferns and softening the hard edges of pavement.

New Guinea Impatiens

The introduction of new hybrid impatiens, derived from plants found in New Guinea in 1970, brought a new look to American gardens. With dark, variegated foliage, bigger flowers, and the ability to tolerate full sun, New Guinea impatiens have found their way into flowerbeds, borders, and hanging baskets across the country.

New Guinea impatiens range from 18 to 26 inches tall and sport lush leaves that may be green, red, or variegated. They have more upright stems than other impatiens, and their blooms are twice the size. In addition to their large, cheerful blooms, these hybrids are outstanding for their lush, colorful foliage; this color must be considered when using New Guinea impatiens in mixed plantings. For example, Constellation has green-and-yellow leaves, while Star War features dark red foliage.

New Guinea impatiens are patented and are propagated from cuttings rather than seeds, so the plants are generally more expensive than other impatiens. However, New Guinea impatiens grow larger than common impatiens, so you should space them 2 feet apart. Thus you will need fewer transplants to fill a bed.

The variegated leaves and lavender flowers of this New Guinea impatiens are a bright foil to dark evergreens.

Different Selections

New selections of impatiens are being continuously developed, causing many different forms, sizes, and colors to be available to gardeners. Dwarf types are great for hanging baskets and ground covers in shady and wooded settings. The Twinkle series produces bicolored flowers with a white central star, and the Super Elfin series comes in many solid colors.

There are dwarf versions of the ever-popular Elfins. Growing about a foot tall in the South, they are very full and spill nicely over the edge of a container. Medium-height impatiens, which are 3 to 4 inches taller than the dwarfs, include the bicolored Ripples series, Tangeglow with bright orange flowers, and Blitz, which has red blooms with bronze foliage and was the first impatiens to win an All-America Selections award.

Among taller impatiens (18 inches and up), look for the Grand series and the Imp series, both with many solid colors. For double-flowered impatiens, which look like tiny roses, consider Fancifrills.

Troubleshooting

Impatiens branch from the base so they seldom grow leggy. However, in the South, plants may grow a third taller than the height stated on the label because they continue to grow during warm nights. To trim them back, snip the tips by no more than one-third. Also, remember that impatiens growing in full morning sun with plenty of water may grow twice as tall as the same selection that gets only an hour of sun per day and less water. Keep this in mind when you choose your selections and planting locations.

Impatiens are often bothered by slugs. Turn to page 236 to read about control of these pests.

Impatiens branch at the base to form dense, compact plants.

Lantana

Lantana softens the landscape with exuberant foliage and masses of bright flowers that attract butterflies.

From early summer until the first freeze, lantana colors the garden with clusters of small flowers that range from bright yellow and orange to pastel rose, lavender, and white. Certain selections behave like chameleons, with their tiny flowers fading and changing color from day to day. Its dependable flowering, lovely form, and tough, woody nature make lantana hard to beat as a summer accent plant.

Lantana is actually a tropical shrub and produces long branches. Some selections creep while others arch upward. Creeping types grow about 1 foot tall and 3 feet wide. Larger arching types may grow to 4 feet tall and equally wide. Both can be planted to soften the hard edges of the landscape, such as marking a patio corner or spilling over a rock wall. This annual is great for the front of the border or as a summer ground cover. You will also appreciate lantana for its ability to attract butterflies.

Lantana's trailing nature makes it perfect for cascading over walls.

AT A GLANCE
❖
LANTANA
Lantana species

Features: bouquetlike clusters of small flowers from summer to fall

Colors: yellow, rose, lavender, orange

Height: 1 to 4 feet tall

Light: full sun

Soil: well drained, average

Water: low to medium

Pests: spider mites, whiteflies

Remarks: forgiving of heat, excellent for containers

Planting and Care

Set out plants in full sun about two weeks after the last frost. Lantana tolerates poor, sandy soil or clay when provided good drainage. It blooms profusely, even in the hottest weather, and is often perennial in the Lower and Coastal South. Water well during extended dry spells to keep the dark green foliage from wilting.

You may overwinter potted lantana indoors in a sunroom or cool garage, but be prepared to control spider mites and whiteflies. Trim the plant back a few weeks before spring planting to encourage branching and fullness.

Different Selections

Lantana *(Lantana camara)* is sold for containers and shrub beds. Most selections grow 3 to 4 feet tall. Radiation, whose flower clusters are yellow, then orange and red, often sports all three colors at the same time. Pink Caprice produces a combination of pink and yellow flower clusters. Dazzler is a tricolor of delicate pink, yellow, and white with an abundance of large flowers. Miss Huff is a more cold-hardy selection that is perennial through the warmer parts of the Middle South. Lemon Swirl is a smaller, 1- to 1½-foot plant with variegated leaves, pale yellow flowers, and a strong scent.

Trailing lantana *(Lantana montevidensis)* is a cascading plant that grows from 12 to 30 inches (depending on the selection). It is popular for containers and hanging baskets where its lilac flowers bloom in profusion. Its stems are thin and lie flat, creeping along the ground or dangling from a basket or over a wall. Try White Lightnin' or Lavender Swirl, or use both together in a basket.

Troubleshooting

Lantana is bothered by spider mites and whiteflies. Spider mites are at their worst during dry weather in spring and fall. Whiteflies usually appear from mid- to late summer. Both pests will cause the leaves to turn a sickly yellow. Turn to page 236 for more information about spider mites and whiteflies.

This lantana's radiant tricolored blossoms are cheerful and attractive to the eye.

Larkspur

Admired for its cool colors and graceful spires, larkspur makes an elegant backdrop.

AT A GLANCE

❖

LARKSPUR
Consolida species

Features: mid- to late spring annual with tall, handsome spires of color

Colors: white, pink, rose, red, blue, lavender, salmon

Height: 1 to 5 feet

Light: full sun to partial shade

Soil: loose, well drained

Water: medium

Pests: slugs

Remarks: excellent cut or dried flower

Sprouting from seed while the weather is cool, larkspur is a charming addition to the spring garden with its old-fashioned colors, airy foliage, and graceful flowering spikes. Amid clouds of light green stems and leaves, 2- to 4-foot-tall spikes shoot up with pink, deep blue, white, and lavender blooms. Though similar in appearance to delphinium, larkspur is easier to grow, especially in the South, where it reseeds and returns annually in a reliable burst of color.

Use larkspur in the middle or back of a border, against a fence, or in a meadow or cutting garden. Its traditional color scheme—pink, white, and blue—mixes beautifully with roses. Blue larkspur brings out the sunny side of golden marigolds, poppies, and calliopsis. Newer salmon colors are lovely with white daisies. When planted with spring-blooming bulbs, larkspur will emerge to conceal the leaves and stems of the other plants with its own fernlike foliage. Larkspur also fills in gaps between spring and summer perennials in a bed. If interplanted with summer-blooming cosmos, the cosmos will bloom furiously as the larkspur finally fades in summer heat.

For centuries, gardeners have enjoyed larkspur for its elegance as a cut flower. Because it retains its rich colors after drying, it is also used in arrangements of dried flowers.

Planting and Care

Larkspur grows best when started from seed directly sown in loose, well-drained soil in full sun or partial shade. In the South, sow larkspur seeds in the fall after the soil has cooled; seeds will not germinate at temperatures above 70 degrees. Plants will sprout in fall and wait through winter, resuming growth with each warm spell as spring approaches. Even if the seeds do not sprout, sowing seed in fall gives plants a chance to sprout early in the spring, which promotes longer flowering. Farther north, you should sow seeds in early spring as soon as the soil is workable. This annual enjoys cool weather when given ample water.

Larkspur is difficult, but not impossible, to transplant. If you want to grow your own transplants, sow seeds in 4-inch pots (one seed per pot) so that the roots will not be disturbed when you transplant them. Place the pots in a cool area. Seeds are slow to germinate, taking about four weeks, so start them six to eight weeks prior to setting out seedlings. Do not start seeds too early; seedlings should be young (1 to 2 inches tall) when transplanted.

Provided the right conditions, larkspur will thrive and reseed from year to year. In times of drought, water once a week. Do not let the plants dry out. In the South, larkspur begins to fade as the weather warms in June, but if you keep it well watered, it will persist a few more weeks.

Different Selections

Larkspur is accurately known by the name *Consolida,* with different species, such as *Consolida ambigua,* branching larkspur, and *Consolida orientalis,* rocket larkspur. In catalogs, however, you may see it labeled *Delphinium ajacis,* which is an outdated scientific name.

Many gardeners have tried-and-true selections of larkspur in their gardens that reseed and return every year. Newer hybrids greatly expand the color palette. Rosamund is a soft rose. Los Angeles Improved is a salmon pink. Blue Spire Improved is a cool dark blue. Giant Imperial remains popular in mixes or with Imperial Blue Bell and Imperial White King. Blue Picotee is a pretty selection with white and lavender flowers. Among low-growing selections is Dwarf Hyacinth Flowered, a rich blue.

Troubleshooting

If you have trouble growing larkspur, your soil may be too acid. Add lime to raise the pH to 7.0 or neutral. You should also watch out for slugs; turn to page 236 to read about this pest.

A classic cottage-garden flower, larkspur is easy to grow and adds an air of nostalgia to beds and borders.

Lisianthus

Large, durable blooms and waxy, blue-gray foliage make for a striking garden display.

Tender-looking but tough, lisianthus is a newcomer to the garden scene. Much appreciated for its tolerance to heat and drought, it prefers poor soil and blooms all summer long in flowerbeds plagued with sandy soil. Lisianthus also thrives in containers.

Although native to Texas, lisianthus was brought to the attention of American gardeners by the Japanese, who hybridized it for the florist trade. The blooms last for weeks, and tall selections are excellent for cutting. Breeding has introduced dwarf versions of this flower for bedding. Fortunately, these newer versions retain the pioneer hardiness of wild lisianthus, also known as Texas Blue Bell.

A mass planting of lisianthus yields a sea of blue, white, or pink. You can also mix it with other annuals or perennials for spots of color. The plant has drought-resistant, waxy foliage that is bluish gray—a handsome companion to the colorful blooms.

AT A GLANCE
❖
LISIANTHUS
Eustoma grandiflorum

Features: large blooms, long flowering, drought tolerant

Colors: pink, white, purplish blue

Height: 6 to 24 inches

Light: full sun

Soil: medium to dry, poor

Water: low to medium

Pests: none specific

Remarks: lasts for weeks as a cut flower

Flowering in profusion, lisianthus softens this formal hedge.

Planting and Care

Like so many plants that can take heat and drought, lisianthus does not like wet conditions. Well-drained soil is a must, making this a perfect annual for poor, sandy soil.

Set plants out in full sun after the last frost. While lisianthus needs little water and fertilizer, it does appreciate having its old blooms removed (which ensures continued blooming until the first fall frost). The foliage will remain all winter in areas seldom hit by frost. In these locations, you may find that lisianthus acts as a perennial, sprouting again from dormant roots provided it has adequate drainage.

Lisianthus does not like acid soil. The pH level of your soil should be nearly neutral, 6.5, for this annual to grow. To raise the pH level, add lime to the soil in the pot or bed.

Different Selections

Lisianthus is seldom started from seed, so you are limited to the selections sold at local garden centers. Many of these are the dwarf types, such as Yodel, or the double-flowered selections, such as Echo, which grow about 24 inches tall and almost equally wide. Both need to be pinched as soon as you plant them to encourage a well-branched plant.

Perfect for a terrace, potted lisianthus thrives during hot summer weather.

Newer selections, such as Blue Lisa, grow less than a foot tall; well branched and compact, they require no pinching. For cutting gardens, seek out the tallest selections, such as Heidi. Tall selections have blossoms concentrated at the top for greater show on longer stems.

Troubleshooting

It is essential to stake long-stemmed selections of lisianthus, or they will be knocked down by storms. Tie them to a stake, or use a three-legged, grow-through support.

Madagascar Periwinkle

Many hybrid Madagascar periwinkle selections are prized for the size and clear color of their blooms.

If there is a bedding plant made for heat waves, it is Madagascar periwinkle. This rugged annual not only survives the scorching heat of July and August, it blooms right through it. In fact, it flowers from spring until the first fall frost. Even in drought, dependable Madagascar periwinkle brings summer color to garden borders, planters, and window boxes.

The blossoms of this hardy annual cover the glossy green mounds of foliage. They can be white, pink, rose, lavender, or, most recently, bright red—in solid colors or splashed at the center with a red, pink, or yellow starlet. Because of its low, spreading nature, Madagascar periwinkle should be planted where it will be easily seen, such as in the foreground of a flower border. The best effect comes from a mass planting in an area at least 10 feet square.

Should space be limited, tuck one or two plants in a location where the flowers can be enjoyed up close, such as along a garden path or beside steps. Also try planting it in containers to bring color to a deck, a terrace, or a patio. In Florida, Madagascar periwinkle grows like a wildflower, and because it is salt tolerant, it is a great plant for gardens near the beach.

Planting and Care

Unlike many annuals, Madagascar periwinkle does not respond well to a lot of water and fertilizer. It will languish in a garden during prolonged wet weather. These plants like poor, slightly dry soil. Either full sun or partial shade is fine, but flowering is better in a sunny location.

In the spring, set out transplants rather than sowing seeds. You can do this about two weeks after the last frost. Never plant too early or Madagascar periwinkle will rot, especially in a wet spring. Even

---

AT A GLANCE

❖

MADAGASCAR PERIWINKLE
Catharanthus roseus

Features: dependable summer color for hot, dry weather

Colors: white, pink, lavender, rose, red

Height: 3 to 20 inches

Light: full sun to partial shade

Soil: slightly dry, poor

Water: low, only when wilting after established

Pests: rot

Remarks: thrives in heat, salt tolerant, great plant for the beach

---

plants set out later may be attacked by rot (fungus) if the weather is wet or there is a lot of dew. If rot becomes a problem, skip a year or two before planting Madagascar periwinkle again.

Water about once a week (count a good rain as a watering) for two to three weeks or until established. Then water only if the plants begin to wilt.

Different Selections

Madagascar periwinkle is generally classified in three groups, based on plant height: bush (also called standard), dwarf, and creeping (sometimes called extra dwarf). The bush types, such as the award-winning Parasol, grow 18 to 20 inches tall and provide a solid mass of color. The Pretty Series has captured attention with another award-winning plant, Pretty in Rose, which boasts large, mauve, velvety flowers with petals overlapping so that there are no gaps.

Catalogs describe the dwarf types as 8 to 10 inches tall; however, they may grow 11 to 14 inches tall in the South. Among dwarf selections are Little Blanche (white flowers), Little Bright Eye (white flowers with a red eye), Little Pinkie (rosy pink), and the Cooler series. Vinca Pacifica Red expands the periwinkle color palette to nearly red.

Creeping types reach a height of only 3 to 5 inches. These bloom only at the ends of the stems, which limits flower production somewhat, but they work well for hanging baskets. Polka Dot is one selection of creeping Madagascar periwinkle.

Window boxes and other full-sun containers offer the perfect summer stage for Madagascar periwinkle.

Starting from Seed

For a fall encore of flowers, you can sow seeds of Madagascar periwinkle in August directly in the garden. Keep them well watered; flowering should begin in about three to four weeks. The plants will reseed, with subsequent blooms often reverting to pink shades. However, transplanting is recommended over seed sowing for the successful cultivation of Madagascar periwinkle.

Marigold

Pure sunset colors and fernlike foliage make marigolds a welcome addition to the summer and fall garden.

AT A GLANCE
❖
MARIGOLD
Tagetes hybrids

Features: brilliant sunset colors for summer and fall

Colors: yellow, orange, burnt red, burgundy, white

Height: 6 to 36 inches

Light: full sun

Soil: average

Water: medium

Pests: spider mites

Remarks: easy to grow from seed

Few garden flowers are more instantly recognizable than marigolds. These bright blossoms of burnt red, deep orange, bright yellow, creamy white, and bicolors have long been popular annuals for late spring and summer color. In the South, gardeners also set them out in late summer as an alternative to mums. Marigolds may be combined with other annuals and perennials in a flowerbed or a pot, and they are popular as spots of color in vegetable gardens. Taller types can serve as filler in a perennial border or even as a background.

One of the easiest ways to use marigolds is in containers on a deck, a terrace, or a patio. Dwarf selections work well in strawberry jars and window boxes; they are also suited for the front of the flower border, as a low edging, and for tight planting areas in rock gardens.

Giant-flowered marigolds are popular for cutting, approaching zinnias in flower size. The tall types also work well as a bold flash of yellow or orange in a summer flowerbed. Because the blooms are like giant medallions, a grouping of only three to five plants can make a good show.

Planting and Care

Marigolds need full sun to flower well and grow best in fertile, moist, well-drained soil. However, they also grow satisfactorily in poor soils, although they will not be as full. After danger of frost is past, sow seed directly in the ground or set out transplants. Transplants may grow slowly at first. The younger the plant, the better it transplants. Space dwarf selections about 6 inches apart, and give taller selections about 12 inches.

Marigolds are moderately drought resistant, but need water during extended dry periods. Dry weather also encourages spider mites. For best results, water marigolds every three or four rainless days, being sure to wet the foliage to discourage spider mites.

Keep plants blooming by pinching off faded flowers throughout the season; if spent blooms are not removed, flowering decreases. Low-growing marigolds tend to become leggy by midsummer and blooms become sparse, especially in areas where night temperatures are high. The quickest and easiest way to rejuvenate these compact plants is to shear them back to about 6 inches high. Continue to trim them to keep them in bloom. Do not cut back taller types; they do not do well when trimmed.

Different Selections

The many popular species of marigolds all originated in the Americas, despite the exotic names given to them by European growers. The African marigold *(Tagetes erecta),* more recently called the American marigold, features large blossoms and leaves. The popular Dwarf French marigold *(Tagetes patula)* blooms early and bears smaller blooms than American marigolds. This plant yields good short-stemmed cut flowers and works well as a potted plant. Triploids, or "3-N" hybrids, are similar to Dwarf French types. They are compact, vigorous plants that are 12 to 16 inches in height and 14 to 20 inches across but bear larger blossoms than Dwarf French marigolds. The term **triploid** refers to an extra set of chromosomes that these plants have, usually resulting in larger blooms.

Signet marigolds *(Tagetes tenuifolia)* sport dainty single blossoms and are great for containers, edgings, and hanging baskets, as these plants do not have the stiff, erect form of other marigolds. Forming low-growing mats (8 to 12 inches in height) of lacy leaves and blossoms, signet marigolds may reach 2 feet or more in diameter. Available in yellow, orange, and gold, they look delightful in any container, especially strawberry jars. They are also slightly frost-tolerant, lasting longer into fall than other marigolds.

When buying transplants or seed, remember that marigolds are also grouped in garden centers by their landscape uses. Edging marigolds (10 inches or less in height) have short, neat forms that are good for outlining beds of taller flowers, bordering sidewalks, and filling containers. Series such as Boy, Janie, Little Devil, and Little Hero are typical of edging types. Spreading marigolds (8 to 12 inches in height), such as signet marigolds, provide a more free-form plant for containers and edgings.

Nothing beats marigolds for quick spots of color, as attested to by these dwarf selections in a strawberry jar.

Pom-pom flowers characterize the larger selections of marigolds.

Marigolds and chrysanthemums mixed with tall grasses create a fireworks of color and texture in the fall garden.

Divider marigolds (11 to 18 inches tall) are used in rows or drifts to divide groups of taller background plants and to provide a backdrop for low-growing edging flowers. Look for names such as Bonanza, Early Spice, Hero, Safari, Discovery, Inca, and Galore.

Background and tall marigolds (19 to 36 inches or more in height) are used in flowerbeds or accent groups, or to fill small beds, corners, and other small areas. They are also good for cutting, as their stems are long enough for use in arrangements. Series include Jubilee, Gold Coin, Climax, French Vanilla, and Snowdrift. Tall marigolds intended for cutting may require staking if they are in an area subject to heavy rain or windstorms.

Starting from Seed

Because they bloom quickly and are so easy to grow, marigolds are among the most popular flowers grown from seed. Scatter seed directly on top of the ground and pat so that it is in firm contact with the soil but never buried. If you choose to start seeds early indoors, sow in pots at least six weeks before the last frost.

Troubleshooting

Spider mites love marigold leaves and can be especially bad in dry weather. Check the underside of leaves before buying bedding plants to make sure that you are not bringing these pests home. See page 236 for more about spider mites.

In some areas of the South, the combination of long days and high temperatures can cause a temporary halt in blooming. Many gardeners work around both problems—halting blooms and spider mites—by planting a second crop of marigolds in late July or August.

Melampodium

Melampodium is a reliable staple of the summer garden. Lush yet drought tolerant, this annual is covered with 1-inch-wide, daisylike flowers and blooms without fail until frost. Planted in full sun or partial shade, it fills out with many branches like a small shrub, providing a bright mass of color ideal for flowerbeds and the edge of wooded areas. It grows up to 18 inches tall and equally wide, with bright green foliage that adds almost as much to the color scheme as the flowers do.

Use melampodium at the base of a mailbox or fence post; this plant can survive with little water and does well in out-of-the-way places. It can soften the abrupt corners of a low deck and steps, as well as the lines of walkways and raised beds. Because it stays neat and solid, it is ideal for borders and rock gardens. Melampodium's flowers are small but numerous and open just above the foliage, creating a nice contrast with larger flowers on long stems, such as daisies, coneflowers, or zinnias. Combine this annual with other yellows, such as lantana or marigold, or let it shine when paired with lilac verbena. It makes a good companion for sun-loving ferns, such as Southern Shield, because it can take a little shade. Melampodium also thrives in large tubs or planters on a deck or a patio.

A gently mounding plant, melampodium is a natural for edging pathways with sunny color and foliage that look good every day from spring until fall.

Planting and Care

Melampodium is easy to grow. For blooms in early summer, set out transplants after the threat of frost is past. Sow seed directly in the garden after the last frost or in late spring for late summer and fall blooms.

Grow your own transplants indoors by sowing seeds two months prior to transplanting time. Water transplants until they are established, and then let nature take care of them. If the mature plants produce a lot of foliage and few blooms, plants may be getting too much shade or too much fertilizer. As for spent blooms, melampodium sheds them on its own, requiring no deadheading to continue blooming. Melampodium reseeds and will surprise you by springing up all over the garden to create new color combinations each summer.

Different Selections

Medallion is the most popular selection, growing 20 to 24 inches tall and boasting sunny golden blooms. In fact, melampodium is sometimes called medallion plant. In the wild, it is known as butter daisy.

AT A GLANCE

❖

MELAMPODIUM
Melampodium paludosum

Features: mounding annual with bright green leaves and yellow blooms

Colors: golden yellow

Height: 18 to 24 inches

Light: full sun to very light shade

Soil: well drained

Water: medium

Pests: none specific

Remarks: foliage is as attractive as blooms

Mexican Mint Marigold

These single blooms have a simple, old-fashioned quality.

Although planted in spring, this annual does not bloom until the fall. However, gardeners can enjoy the attractive green foliage of Mexican mint marigold in the interim. Established plants bear an occasional flower in the spring but bloom profusely in the fall. When the plant finally blooms, flowers top 1- to 2-foot-tall stems.

The feathery foliage of Mexican mint marigold resembles that of the culinary herb French tarragon, which does not grow in hot, humid climates. Herb gardeners across the South have discovered that they can substitute this heat-tolerant, anise-scented plant in recipes that need the flavor of tarragon. You can snip fresh sprigs as needed, beginning in spring. Or simply enjoy the color and form of this handsome herb. Known as mint marigold in Texas, this annual is called Mexican tarragon by Floridians, and sweet-scented marigold and Spanish tarragon by others.

Combine Mexican mint marigold with chrysanthemums in a flowerbed, or let it be a bright spot in your herb garden, which often looks tired by summer's end. Although grown as an annual in most of the country, Mexican mint marigold behaves as a half-hardy perennial in warmer regions. With regular, light frosts in the Lower South, it dies above ground, but if mulched, the roots will survive overnight dips as low as 5 degrees. In the southern tips of Florida and Texas, it never dies down.

Planting and Care

Mexican mint marigold is available as seeds or transplants. It grows in full sun and in partial shade but demands well-drained soil. Once established, it spreads from stems that root when they fall to the ground; propagate young plants to bring indoors for winter by rooting stems. In areas with hard winters, plant in the spring. However, transplants set in Coastal South gardens in the fall develop root systems during the winter and grow vigorously in spring.

The yellow flowers of Mexican mint marigold are a showy addition to fall flower gardens.

Morning Glory and Moonflower

Morning glories provide quick summer color for fences, porches, or trellises.

Two closely related vines, morning glory (*Ipomoea purpurea*) and moonflower (*Ipomoea alba*), refresh the garden with their lush, heart-shaped foliage and broad, saucerlike flowers from early summer until the first frost. Given full sun and regular watering, these vigorous vines thrive in heat, growing a foot or more per week, to stretch across a handrail or a fence in little time. Few plants reward the gardener with better value. One packet of seeds is enough to envelop an entire garden in glorious lengths of blooming vine.

Morning glory and moonflower make a great pair. Morning glory blooms in the morning, with its delicate blossoms closing by midday. A few hours later, the fragrant moonflower opens its lovely white blooms and perfumes the air. Plant them around any vertical structure: the post of a mailbox, a fence, an arbor, or the supports of a porch or a deck. They will grow in large pots if given frequent water and something to climb. Because they grow quickly and live only one season, these vines can be planted where a more slow-growing perennial will eventually be, filling an otherwise blank space.

Morning Glory

Morning glory vines will twine to lengths of 8 to 10 feet or more, providing profuse and continuous flowers in shades of blue, pink, lavender, or crimson. Although the blooms are open to greet you only in the morning, the plant itself is wonderfully rugged, thriving in heavy clay or poor sand along roadsides all over the country. It will twine and climb a support, or sprawl as a ground cover where there is nothing to climb. You can also create lovely combinations, pairing morning glory with other vines, such as the tropical mandevilla or fall-blooming clematis.

Moonflower

This vine could be called evening glory, as it comes to life when the sun sets. Its large, saucer-shaped blooms unfurl quickly, often in less than a minute, in late afternoon. They are a treat for anyone,

---

AT A GLANCE

❖

MORNING GLORY
Ipomoea purpurea

Features: old-fashioned, showy summer vine for morning

Colors: blue, lilac, rose, purple, magenta, white, striped, bicolored

Height: 8 to 10 feet

Light: full sun

Soil: rich to poor and sandy

Water: medium to low

Pests: none specific

Remarks: fast growing

---

especially children. Aptly named, moonflower's broad blooms reflect moonlight, making it a great choice for planting around patios and decks where you spend time on summer evenings. The blooms are also sweetly fragrant and attract large sphinx moths that flutter like hummingbirds. Moonflower is very vigorous, growing 10 to 15 feet or more; this vine is capable of overtaking nearby plants, so it is best used alone or combined with vines that are equally vigorous.

Planting and Care

Morning glory and moonflower grow best when started from seed sown directly in the garden. Plant in full sun after all danger of frost has passed. Nick the hard coat of the seeds with a nail file and soak in a pan of water for several hours. Morning glory and moonflower are not picky about their soil, growing in rich or poor ground. Water plants until they are well established. After that, they are drought tolerant, but the leaves will temporarily wilt at the height of a scorching summer day.

If you want to plant these vines along a fence, plant two seeds (inches apart) every 4 to 5 feet and train young vines in opposite directions. The vines are likely to grow out of hand in a small-scale planting, such as around a mailbox, so be prepared to cut them back. Otherwise, give them a sturdy support with plenty of room to roam. They will grow and twist up a small trellis, but you will need to use twine or other supports to keep the vines on lampposts, columns, or other large, smooth structures. Both morning glory and moonflower bloom longer if you deadhead old blooms to keep seed pods from forming.

Different Selections

For morning glory, Heavenly Blue remains one of the most popular selections, with its sky blue color fading to white toward the center of 5-inch-wide flowers. Sunrise Mixed features an array of striped and bicolored flowers in pink, purple, rose, lilac, sky blue, and white. Scarlett O'Hara is an All-America Selections winner with rich crimson flowers. Tall Mixed contains a range of colors and climbs higher than other selections. Crimson Rambler produces deep magenta flowers that are attractive to hummingbirds.

There are few named selections of moonflower. Giant White is one selection frequently found in seed catalogs. All moonflowers boast fragrant, white flowers that may be 6 inches across.

AT A GLANCE

❖

MOONFLOWER
Ipomoea alba

Features: summer vine that blooms at night
Colors: white
Height: 10 to 15 feet
Light: full sun
Soil: rich to poor and sandy
Water: medium
Pests: none specific
Remarks: fast growing, fragrant

Moonflower unfurls quickly in late afternoon; plant it where you can enjoy its sweet fragrance.

Moss Rose and Purslane

The pure, bright flowers of purslane bask in the sun but stay closed on cloudy days.

Moss rose is named for the roselike fullness of its blooms.

Moss rose and purslane earn their keep in the heat of summer. Both plants have drought-tolerant, succulent leaves and do not grow or bloom well until the weather warms up in late spring. Old-fashioned moss rose bears delicate, roselike blossoms in soft shades of orange, red, yellow, pink, and white. Its succulent leaves are gray green and needlelike, and the plants spread up to 2 feet wide and 4 to 6 inches tall. Moss rose is good for beds, rock gardens, rock walls, and containers, but its stems are too brittle for hanging baskets.

Purslane is a hybrid that is often sold in hanging baskets. It has single flowers and spoon-shaped leaves on trailing stems. (This is not the same plant as the weedy, yellow-flowered purslane that invades lawns and pastures.)

Because of their succulent leaves and stems, moss rose and purslane are nearly as tolerant of summer heat as cacti. They like to bask in the sun, opening their flowers in the morning and closing them in the heat of the afternoon. On extremely hot days, the blooms may close by noon, especially if the soil is dry. On cloudy days, flowers are slow to open or may remain closed.

Use moss rose and purslane anywhere a low-growing, creeping flower will do well—edgings, beds, rock gardens, dry banks, and between paving stones. Because of their brightly colored blossoms, they make a great summer ground cover. Their tolerance of drought makes them good choices for containers, too.

Purslane makes a great summer container plant.

AT A GLANCE
❖
MOSS ROSE AND PURSLANE
Portulaca species and hybrids

Features: creeping, drought-tolerant mat with colorful summer blooms

Colors: yellow, white, pink, red, purple, salmon

Height: 2 to 6 inches

Light: full sun

Soil: well drained; average, rocky, or sandy

Water: low

Pests: none specific

Remarks: tolerates sun and poor soil

Planting and Care

Well-drained soil is a must. These plants do well in sandy soil and are great for gardens near the beach. After the danger of frost has passed, moss rose can be started from transplants, but it sprouts easily from seed, too. Purslane is sold as transplants or as established plants in hanging baskets. It is grown only from cuttings, either commercially propagated in a greenhouse or from a plant that you have saved; seed is not available.

Although they are very drought tolerant, young plants should be watered and fertilized to encourage quick growth. Cut plants back by about one-third if they creep out of bounds. Keep hanging baskets of purslane full in the center by cutting a few of the branches back every month. Snipping off old blooms keeps the plants blooming until the first cold snap.

Purslane forms a dense, colorful summer ground cover.

Different Selections

Moss rose selections include the Sundial series, one of the first to allow you to choose one specific color. (Most selections are sold as a multicolored mix.) Minilaca is named for its extremely compact 2-inch plants that stay short and do not spread. Purslane is rarely sold by selection name but rather by color; seed is not available, so you will not find it listed in seed catalogs.

Starting from Seed

Moss rose (not purslane) is easy to start from seed. Sow after the last frost. The seeds are tiny; just scatter them in the soil, between stones, or wherever you would like a blooming ground cover. Keep seeds watered until plants germinate and become established. It will be two months before blooms appear.

Moss rose spills its blooms into a walkway.

Pansy, Viola, and Johnny-Jump-Up

Yellow pansies make blues and purples appear brighter.

Pansy, viola, and Johnny-jump-up are related flowers prized for fall, winter, and spring color. Botanically, all are *Viola* species, and each will delight you with a variety of colors and uses. Although all are low growing, the main differences among the three are the size of the leaves and the blooms, which allow you to fine-tune their uses in the landscape.

In the South, few bedding plants can hold their own against the changing seasons like these do. Plant a group in the fall, and they will bloom right away. Give the plants light mulch for protection, and they will bloom in winter, with each warm spell bringing out a splash of color. By spring, they are finally free to bloom like never before. Flowers cover the plants throughout March and April before they begin fading in the heat.

Pansy

Pansies *(Viola x Wittrockiana)* boast the largest plants and blooms of this group, but they are still rather low, generally growing only 4 to 8 inches tall. Because they are low growing, pansies are ideal for planting in the front of a border or in a bed beside a terrace or walk. If they become lanky and flop or spill from their beds, you can trim them back a few inches. They are also striking when massed in a single color in formal beds.

Pansies are great companions for other flowers, especially early spring bulbs, such as daffodils and tulips. Through winter, pansies

The front of a tulip border is an ideal place for pansies.

bring color that is close to the ground, and in spring, the bulbs provide another level of colorful blooms above. Pansies also make lovely companions for iris, filling out the bed in winter. A row of tall pastel foxgloves behind a solid row of blue pansies can make an elegant impression. They also mingle well with ivy in containers. Some pansies have a delicate perfume that adds a slight fragrance in addition to charming color.

Do not be concerned that pansies will fade when the weather turns cold; many selections tolerate temperatures as low as 15 degrees.

Viola

Violas (*Viola cornuta*) are often called minipansies because they look so much like small pansies. The smaller scale of their leaves, stems, and flowers makes them perfect for pots from fall through spring. Violas seldom flop over like pansies and are perfect for pots in combination with spring bulbs. The smaller size of these blooms is reminiscent of violets.

Johnny-Jump-Up

The smallest of the group, Johnny-jump-up (*Viola tricolor*), is also known as Good King Henry. Plant in fall to enjoy early spring flowers. They prefer partial shade and rich, well-drained soil. They often reseed, so they return each year. Plant Johnny-jump-ups in a quiet spot near steps, an entryway, or on the edge of a wooded garden. They like to reseed between stones, in gravel, or between cracks in pavement. Colors range from white and lemon yellow to violet blue and tricolors of violet, lavender, and yellow.

Different Selections

Pansies come in three different classifications based largely on size of bloom: large (3½ to 4½ inches), medium (2½ to 3½ inches), and multiflora (1½ to 2½ inches). Among large pansies are Swiss Giant, Accord, and Majestic Giant series; because of their size, they are also popular as cut flowers. Medium-sized pansies include Crown (all solid colors), Joker, Roc, and Imperial series, perfect for pots or bedding. The Imperial series is prized for its vigorous growth and unique shades, particularly pink. Multiflora types are also called landscape pansies because they bloom so profusely in wide swaths. Although the blossoms are smaller than those of other pansies, they produce so many blooms that it is difficult to see their foliage. They are more

Joker Light Blue vibrates with color.

A white pansy mixes well with all colors and looks lovely at night.

Imperial Orange Prince, an All-America Selections winner, is noted for its color.

Pansy, Viola, and Johnny-Jump-Up

Violas offer smaller, more delicate blooms than pansies.

heat tolerant, lasting until the final days of spring. Noteworthy selections include Universal, Maxim, and Crystal Bowl series and Padparadja, an unusual orange.

Violas are available in all the same colors as pansies. Some have a white throat or a yellow eye in the center of the flower. The Jewel and Princess series offer 1-inch blooms in yellow, white, and shades of purple.

AT A GLANCE

❖

VIOLA
Viola cornuta

Features: small pansylike blooms

Colors: white, violet, lavender, yellow

Height: 7 inches

Light: full sun

Soil: rich, well drained

Water: medium

Pests: slugs

Remarks: great for pots

The deep yellow blossoms of Universal Hybrid pansies bring out the yellow centers of Shasta daisies.

The Alpine Summer series of Johnny-jump-up features tricolored blooms of yellow, light blue, and dark blue. Blue Elf has flowers of violet blue, and Helen Mount combines violet, lavender, and yellow in a single bloom.

Planting and Care

Fall is the time to plant pansies, violas, and Johnny-jump-ups in the South; they grow to twice the size and produce more flowers than those planted in the spring. Spring-planted pansies do not have time to become well established before they start blooming. Colder climates call for spring planting, but pansies there last much later into the summer than they do in the South because of the cooler nights.

Plants need at least six hours of sun; plants in shade produce fewer blooms. Set transplants 6 to 8 inches apart, and water regularly when the weather is dry. In late winter, reapply a controlled-release flower food (see pages 43 and 44). Be sure to keep the plants watered; although forgiving and quick to spring back from wilting, plants will bloom better if the soil is kept moist. As the weather gets hot in the summer, flowers get smaller and plants look weak and stressed. Replace them with annuals that can beat the heat.

Troubleshooting

Slugs often attack the succulent growth of these plants, chewing holes in both the flowers and the foliage. Turn to page 236 for more information about slugs.

Johnny-jump-ups will reseed and spring back again every year.

AT A GLANCE
❖
JOHNNY-JUMP-UP
Viola tricolor

Features: early spring flowers that are smaller than pansies
Colors: blue, tricolored (violet, lavender, yellow)
Height: 7 inches
Light: partial shade
Soil: rich, well drained
Water: medium
Pests: slugs
Remarks: will reseed

Pots of yellow pansies are glowing spots of color. Planted in the fall, they will overwinter in pots in warmer zones.

Petunia

Petunias can be solid or bicolored.

Unlike most annuals, which are either cool- or warm-weather plants, petunias are a little bit of both. Although you see them sold mostly in spring for summer bedding, they are actually great annuals for fall or even winter in the Coastal and Lower South.

Mix petunias with other plants in flowerbeds, mass them for a sea of color, or use them as cascading accents in a mixed pot of annuals. Spreading types also make a unique seasonal ground cover. Pastel and white petunias are especially nice in the evening because their large, disklike blooms reflect moonlight and night lighting.

Planting and Care

The best way to start petunias is from transplants set out in early spring, or in late summer for a fall show. Plant in full sun and in well-drained soil. Petunias do well in poor, sandy soil and tolerate heavy clay and alkaline soil as long as it is well drained.

In the Lower and Coastal South, plant petunias in fall for blooms through three seasons. Choose a selection that is heat tolerant and keep the plants well tended to see blooms from winter until the following summer. Many selections tolerate light frost with no damage; if you live beyond coastal areas, experiment to see how long a fall planting will bloom before it is killed by a hard freeze. In the Upper and Middle South, plant petunias in spring after the last frost for blooms until the first hard freeze.

To keep plants lush and blooming profusely, trim them back an inch or two when they reach 6 inches tall. Transplants are often this tall when purchased; if so, pinch them at planting time. As the plants grow, continue pinching off old blooms to encourage more blooms and branching. Feed the plants again with controlled-release plant food in mid- to late summer. If the plants have grown leggy by mid-summer, prune them back to about one-half their height; then water and fertilize as if they were newly planted. This encourages a new flush of both foliage and flowers for spring.

Different Selections

You will find subtle variety among petunia selections, each with its own strengths. A few selections are fragrant, often releasing their perfume at night to attract moths, which then pollinate the flowers. Many petunias have double, frilled blooms, and some are more heat tolerant than others. Choose a selection that suits your garden's needs.

Grandiflora petunias grow about 8 inches tall and produce the largest blooms, 4 to 5 inches in diameter. These are very showy in pots and baskets. However, they are the most likely to be battered by rain and do not like hot weather. In the South, consider these only for fall or early spring. Grandiflora types include deeply ruffled blooms, such as Can Can, and double blooms, such as Purple Pirouette. Double petunias will need extra fertilizer to develop their extra-large blossoms; feed them with liquid food every third watering.

Multiflora petunias grow about 8 inches tall and have smaller blooms than grandiflora petunias, but more of them. They are more tolerant of hot weather than the giant-flowered grandiflora types. Multiflora petunias will last through summer even in the South if trimmed back and watered and fertilized properly. Primetime is a popular Multiflora series. These plants stay fairly compact even in hot weather. Colors include pink, red, salmon, blue, and white.

Floribunda petunias also have good tolerance to heat. Proven series include Madness, which will survive summer in the South if trimmed back and kept watered and fertilized. The Madness series is available in the standard range of petunia colors and includes double-flowered types. Another proven series is Celebrity, which includes 2- to 3-inch blooms of white and shades of pink, purple, and red.

Double-flowered petunias are more finicky than single blooms but are nonetheless popular for their unusual fullness. This one is Purple Pirouette.

Cascading petunias are ground-hugging plants that grow only 4 to 6 inches tall but may be 36 inches wide. Cascading petunias, such as Supertunia, Cascadia, and Purple Wave, are popular for hanging baskets and as a seasonal ground cover.

Seeds and seedlings of old-fashioned single types, many without names, are often passed among gardeners. These 12- to 18-inch-tall plants are very rugged, establishing themselves in one place and reappearing year after year, even in sandy soil. They bear single blooms in shades of pink and lavender.

The floppy stems of petunias make these annuals perfect for low window boxes, where they can be easily watered, trimmed, and fertilized for a long-lasting show.

Single, old-fashioned petunias are among the most rugged selections and will often reseed themselves.

Poppy

Shirley poppies bloom in an array of colors with interesting markings.

Though fragile in appearance, poppies are quite tough plants whose tufts of foliage are not bothered by cold and whose flowers dance in a spring breeze. Whether massed for solid color or mixed with other annuals and perennials, they animate beds and borders with their paperlike petals in both soft and bright colors. There are several species of annual poppies, but all share the same graceful flowers and similar appearance; once started in a garden, all keep themselves going by reseeding year after year.

Shirley Poppy

The annual Shirley poppy blooms in bright colors atop lanky stems that grow to 3 feet tall. These flowers have yellow or white centers with pink, rose, scarlet, or salmon petals. You can also find bicolored and double-flowered forms. And like their wild relatives, which were brought back by World War I soldiers from Flanders in northwest Europe, Shirley poppies develop strong plants wherever their seeds fall. They will reseed from one year to the next in soil that is left uncultivated and free of mulch.

To grow Shirley poppies, you can set out transplants in spring, but it is easier to sow seeds directly into the garden in early fall or late winter. If planted in fall, plants sprout but stay small through winter and then begin to grow as the weather gets warmer in spring.

AT A GLANCE
❖
SHIRLEY POPPY
Papaver rhoeas

Features: showy blooms for beds, borders, and bouquets
Colors: white, pink, lilac, orange, yellow, red
Height: 1 to 3 feet
Light: full sun
Soil: average, well drained
Water: medium
Pests: none specific
Remarks: reseeds easily

Because of their thin, wispy stems, Shirley poppies look best when planted in large masses.

Iceland Poppy

Another poppy you can sow directly in the garden in fall is Iceland poppy *(Papaver nudicaule)*. Although it is biennial, Iceland poppy will sometimes behave like a perennial when planted in cool regions. It dies down after blooming in spring and then resumes growth in the fall. The foliage is hardy enough to remain green during the mild winters of the South, making Iceland poppy a great annual to plant in fall. It will bloom in spring, but it will not survive the hot, humid summer.

Unlike other poppies, Iceland poppies do not have leaves on their stems; this makes them terrific for use in arrangements of cut flowers. Cut them in the morning just as their blooms open. The flowers will continue to develop once in water. Before arranging cut poppies with other flowers, sear the ends of the stems with a flame or plunge them into boiling water for about 20 seconds to stop the leakage of white sap. Then place them in deep water for a minimum of four hours to get them in good condition for arranging.

AT A GLANCE

❖

ICELAND POPPY
Papaver nudicaule

Features: showy blooms for beds, borders, and bouquets

Colors: white, pink, lilac, orange, yellow, red

Height: 1 to 3 feet

Light: full sun

Soil: average, well drained

Water: medium

Pests: none specific

Remarks: reseeds easily

Iceland poppies come in a variety of colors, including this bright, sunny yellow.

California Poppy

California poppies *(Eschscholzia californica)* are known for their soft, breeze-blown flowers that look beautiful when planted in masses to mimic their presence in the wild. This poppy is native to the West and prefers alkaline soil, making it a good choice for Texas and other areas where the soil pH is high.

Although perennial in its home state, California poppy is grown as an annual in the South. Sow seeds in fall, as they need cool weather to germinate. California poppies also need a lot of water to sprout. If the seed bed dries during the critical two to three week germination period, the seeds will not sprout. If you do not have alkaline soil, add lime to the soil a few weeks before planting to raise the soil pH to 7.0 or higher.

Opium Poppy

Long-time gardeners may know opium poppy *(Papaver somniferum)* quite well. It is one of the best poppies for the South and is often found in old gardens. Opium poppy is prized for its blooms, which may be various shades of pink or white. Some types have double blooms and are called peony flowered; double poppies with fringed petals are referred to as carnation flowered. In addition to its handsome blooms, this poppy also has beautiful waxy blue foliage and is one of the most heat tolerant of all poppies, lasting into late spring and early summer.

Different Selections

One of the available selections of Shirley poppy, Mother of Pearl, offers delicate shades of soft blue, lilac, pink, white, and peach on plants that grow about 3 feet tall. All-Double Shirley bears double flowers on 2-foot plants in white, rose, salmon, and red.

Among Iceland poppies, Champagne Bubbles provides a good mix of solids and some bicolored blooms on full plants, about 1 foot tall. Wonderland is another low-growing selection (12 to 14 inches) that works well as a bedding plant. It has large flowers on short, sturdy stems.

California poppies are known for their natural orange hue, but breeders have developed selections that include yellow, red, pinks, and white. Ballerina Mixed boasts flowers up to 3 inches wide on 1-foot-tall plants.

The thin petals of poppies are nearly translucent. Here they glow among purple and pink bachelor's buttons in a field of color.

Opium poppy is an heirloom, and seeds are often passed among gardeners with no reference to an official and lasting name. However, seed catalogs do list a few selections. Peony-Flowered Oase is named for its fringed double blooms of bright scarlet that resemble peonies. White Cloud bears extra-double white blooms. Hens and Chicks is grown for its sturdy, extra-large seed pods for use in crafts.

Planting and Care

All of the poppies described here can be started from seed directly in the garden in fall or late winter in the South, and in early spring in areas with colder winters. All need full sun and soil with excellent drainage; without good drainage, the plants will rot in winter.

The seeds are small (like the poppy seeds sprinkled on foods). Mix them with a little sand before you sow, or put them in an old kitchen poppy-seed container and use it as a dispenser. Then you can sprinkle seeds evenly over the area. Let the seeds sit on top of the ground, and keep them moist with daily waterings.

Although poppies resent transplanting, you can grow them in containers to be planted in the garden if you transplant while the seedlings are very young (about 1 or 2 inches in diameter). Set transplants 8 to 10 inches apart. Even poppies that reseed themselves need thinning; otherwise, the plants may become so crowded that their stems grow weak enough to be knocked down by hard rain.

Double-flowered selections wear their petals like a skirt of many layers.

AT A GLANCE

❖

OPIUM POPPY
Papaver somniferum

Features: showy spring blooms for beds and borders
Colors: white, pink
Height: 3 feet
Light: full sun
Soil: average, well drained
Water: medium
Pests: none specific
Remarks: reseeds easily

Poppy buds are nearly as attractive as the full blooms.

Rose Verbena

Drought-tolerant rose verbena is forgiving should you forget to water, making it a good choice for containers.

Rose verbena shakes off heat and humidity, welcoming summer and spreading like a ground cover in even the most sultry climates. A Southern native, rose verbena is a low-growing, creeping plant that is covered from midspring to fall in clusters of tiny, velvety pink, white, or purple flowers and finely cut, dark leaves.

Ranging from 6 to 24 inches tall, rose verbena has a niche in summer in flowerbeds and borders, especially those in full sun. Its open, branching foliage permits other plants to grow up around and through it. Rose verbena works well when planted with bulbs, disguising their leaves as they fade. Plant purple selections behind yellow marigolds, coreopsis, or coneflowers around a mailbox or in a perennial border. Or allow it to creep onto the edge of a walkway, add color and texture to a rock garden, or perk up a container of less vivid plants.

Mix rose verbena with yellow lantana or pink petunias in a window box or hanging basket to attract hummingbirds and butterflies. Plant it with Lance Whorton caladiums, which can take more sun than most caladiums, or with any other sun lover to bring a reliable touch of color to the sunniest areas of your garden.

Rose verbena softly spills over this wall as it would over a rocky bank in the wild.

AT A GLANCE

❖

ROSE VERBENA
Verbena canadensis

Features: heat-tolerant, low-spreading plant covered with blooms

Colors: hot pink, deep purple, violet, white

Height: 6 to 24 inches

Light: full sun

Soil: well drained

Water: medium

Pests: spider mites and whiteflies during dry weather

Remarks: drought tolerant, good for containers

Planting and Care

Set out transplants in full sun after all danger of frost has passed. Rose verbena enjoys well-drained garden soil and does very well in poor, sandy soil. Plants quickly form a wavy, loose-knit carpet of flowers, so set them 20 to 24 inches apart. Remove faded flowers to encourage fresh blooms; you may also need to cut back plants during the summer when they become leggy.

Rose verbena can be grown as a short-lived perennial in the Lower and Coastal South and warmer portions of the Middle South. Elsewhere, it is a warm-weather annual, thriving from late spring until the first frost.

Different Selections

The lightly fragrant Homestead Purple sports rich purple blooms and grassy green foliage and is an excellent performer. Abbeville has fragrant, lavender blooms.

While not as hardy as its native cousin, trailing verbena also functions well in summer baskets and in edgings. It features several named selections, including Imagination, with deep violet spring-to-fall flowers, and Sissinghurst, with rose-pink blooms.

Troubleshooting

Spider mites and whiteflies love verbena. Although the plants are tough enough to endure infestations without pesticides, the foliage of plants under attack will be mottled, losing the characteristic dark green sheen. Turn to page 236 for more about these pests.

Rose verbena may be found in several shades of pink and purple.

Scarlet Sage

When planted in a mass under the light shade of pines, scarlet sage looks like wildflowers.

Scarlet sage is one of a kind for summer. Its flower spikes are strong and vertical and combine well with plants that have flat, round flowers and a mounding or horizontal form. Because its drama can overpower other flowers, pair it with something that can match its energy. Yellow marigolds and red or purple scarlet sage will make a vivid combination from late spring until the first frost. Used with a silver-leafed plant, such as dusty miller or artemisia, its red stands alone. White flowers, such as petunias and impatiens, are nice foils to the brilliance of scarlet sage.

Scarlet sage is also effective when planted in a bold, solid mass. Plant a group of at least a dozen plants to create a dense sweep of color. A naturalistic landscape showcases the open-flowering habit of the individual plants best. Plant small groups of scarlet sage beneath pines for a colorful effect reminiscent of wildflowers. Compact selections are suitable for containers, too.

Planting and Care

Set out transplants of scarlet sage in spring, after the danger of frost has passed. Red selections do well in full sun and in partial shade, but white, purple, and rose selections may scorch in the sun. These definitely need partial shade.

All selections of scarlet sage like fertile, well-drained soil. Plants will not flower without water, so water regularly during periods of dry weather. Snip off old flower spikes as they fade to keep the plants compact and to encourage continued flowering until frost. To promote compact, multibranched plants, pinch transplants as soon as you set them out.

Different Selections

Despite the name, not all selections of scarlet sage are red. White, rose, salmon, and purple selections are also available. Selections range from 8 inches to more than 30 inches tall, with the low-growing ones flowering earliest in the season and the tallest beginning about a month later. Use low-growing selections (8 to 12 inches tall), such as Flamenco and Red Hot Sally, at the edge of a border or in a small pot. Plants growing from 14 to 20 inches include Top Burgundy and Blaze of Fire. The tallest ones grow to 24 to 30 inches and include Bonfire, America, and Splendens Tall. In the South, plants may grow 4 to 6 inches taller than the label states, especially in the shade.

AT A GLANCE

❖

SCARLET SAGE
Salvia splendens

Features: masses of intense color with rich foliage

Colors: red, rose, salmon, purple, white

Height: 8 to 30 inches

Light: full sun to partial shade

Soil: fertile, well drained

Water: medium

Pests: none specific

Remarks: vivid colors for natural landscapes

You will see two similar plants, *Salvia coccinea* (Texas sage) and *Salvia elegans* (pineapple sage), for sale in garden centers and catalogs. Although perennial in the Lower and Coastal South, they are annual in the rest of the country. Lady in Red is the most popular selection of *Salvia coccinea*, growing to about 3 feet tall and equally wide. Pineapple sage is sold as an herb because of its scented foliage. Both of these annuals attract hummingbirds.

Another salvia that behaves as an annual in most of the country, but is a short-lived perennial in the Lower and Coastal South, is mealy-cup sage *(Salvia farinacea)*. It produces spikes of deep blue flowers from late spring that will continue through summer if you remove the faded blossoms. Mealy-cup sage may thrive for two or three years in a sunny, well-drained site in the Lower and Coastal South.

The red blooms of pineapple sage are smaller than those of scarlet sage.

Scarlet sage is one of the summer's showiest annuals. Here, a salmon selection continues into fall in combination with wild ageratum, salvia, goldenrod, and chrysanthemums.

Snapdragon

Tall, colorful snapdragons make great back-of-the-border plants when contrasted with lower flowers, such as petunias.

Along with their ice cream colors and frilly flowers, snapdragons are treasured for their strong vertical lines in a flowerbed. Snapdragons, or snaps as they are often called, like cool weather and bring dependable color from winter through spring in the Lower and Coastal South. Farther north, they come alive in spring and summer gardens as spikes of vivid color. They contrast beautifully with other flowers, especially those that hold their blooms horizontally, such as Shasta daisies.

You can mass snapdragons in waves for a solid watercolored effect, plant tall ones as a backdrop for a border, or vary them with lower mounding plants. They also mix well with other colors, as in the marriage of bright yellow snaps and Shasta daisies, or pastel snaps and soft shades of pansies. Dwarf snaps are low-mounding plants that are excellent as edging, fillers in perennial beds, and accents in containers. Taller snaps make excellent cut flowers, lasting a week or more in a vase.

Snapdragons are also fun for children, who can pull down the lower half of the bloom to reveal its mouthlike center. When let go, the flower snaps shut, hence the name.

Planting and Care

In the Coastal and Lower South and in warmer parts of the Middle South, set out young transplants in the fall to give them time to establish themselves before cold weather hits. In cooler areas, set out transplants in early spring.

Snaps like fertile, well-drained soil in full sun but tolerate light shade, though they flower less profusely in it. Water during periods of dry weather, or the plants will not grow to their full size and flower height.

With the exception of dwarf types, each plant first forms a tall flower spike in the center. When this initial spike fades, cut it off at the base and smaller side spikes will appear. Snaps stop blooming if their flowers, which form seed, are not removed. You can also encourage plants to form more spikes from the beginning by pinching the tops off young transplants when you first set them out; these secondary spikes will be smaller than the first.

AT A GLANCE

❖

SNAPDRAGON
Antirrhinum majus

Features: old-fashioned favorite that blooms during the cool season

Colors: yellow, white, pink, red, maroon, orange, bronze, bicolored

Height: 6 to 36 inches

Light: full sun to very light shade

Soil: fertile, well drained, neutral

Water: medium

Pests: none specific

Remarks: tall selections make great cut flowers

Taller types, which are popular for cutting, need to be staked with a grow-through support, stick, or tomato cage. In the South, snaps bloom about a month longer than pansies in the summer before they need to be pulled up. Keep them blooming as long as possible by pinching old blooms and watering regularly.

You can grow snapdragons from seed, but the seed is very small and hard to sow. Transplants grown from seed need nearly four months until flowering starts; it may be hard to keep them cool enough in summer to be ready for fall planting. Your snaps may grow best when started from purchased transplants.

Different Selections

Snapdragons come in three heights, each suited to a particular garden use. Colors may be vivid or pastel and range from white, yellow, and orange to rose, red, bronze, and bicolored. Dwarf selections, such as Tahiti and Pixie, grow 6 to 15 inches tall to provide mounds of color.

Medium to tall selections grow 16 to 30 inches in height and include Liberty, Madame Butterfly, Princess, and Sonnet. Often these form secondary side spikes that flower later than the central, taller spike, thereby extending the length of blooming time and the fullness of the plant.

The tallest snapdragons grow from 24 to 36 inches high and include Bright Butterflies, Panorama, and Rocket. All are prized for cutting and for their strikingly colorful, vertical spikes in beds and, particularly, borders.

Snapdragons offer a full range of color, from bright yellows, reds, and oranges to pastel pinks and pure white.

Snow-on-the-Mountain

Snow-on-the-mountain leaves are gray green with white variegation.

AT A GLANCE
❖
SNOW-ON-THE-MOUNTAIN
Euphorbia marginata

Features: cool, fresh variegated foliage in summer

Colors: gray-green leaves rimmed with white

Height: 1½ to 3 feet

Light: full sun to partial shade

Soil: average to poor, well drained

Water: low to medium

Pests: none specific

Remarks: native wildflower, reseeds prolifically

The gray-green leaves of snow-on-the-mountain are rimmed with white, as if tipped with frost. However, they are merely a cool illusion during the blistering summer. When some annuals suffer in the heat of summer, along comes snow-on-the-mountain, a tenacious, reseeding annual that grows wild from the Dakotas to Texas and thrives in any soil in full sun or partial shade.

This annual, grown for its reliable, variegated foliage, adds stability to a perennial bed as the other plants wax and wane. Its showy green-and-white leaves also help blend the colors of neighboring plants and tone down nearby bright blooms. For a lovely, old-fashioned effect, combine snow-on-the-mountain with spider flower. Although the foliage has the greatest visual impact, you will find dainty white flowers at the tip of each branch. Later these flowers are replaced by a cluster of round pods that hold the promise of snow-on-the-mountain next spring.

Planting and Care

Plant snow-on-the-mountain any time between the last spring frost and midsummer. Choose a sunny, well-drained location. This annual is difficult to transplant; the best way to plant is to sow the seed directly into the garden soil. When seedlings emerge, they will not be variegated like the mature plant but will be gray green in color. Thin seedlings to 1 to 1½ feet apart. The variegation will appear after the seedlings begin to branch out.

Snow-on-the-mountain has a milky sap like that of its relative, poinsettia. The foliage is lovely in arrangements of summer flowers, but the cut ends of the stems must be seared in a flame to stop the sap from running. If you have sensitive skin, be careful when handling the stems; the sap can be irritating.

Different Selections

Although snow-on-the-mountain will generally grow to a height of about 3 feet, a selection called Summer Icicle is only 1½ feet tall.

Troubleshooting

Once you plant snow-on-the-mountain, you must be willing to pull up unwanted seedlings. This annual will reappear at will throughout your garden. Be prepared to pull volunteer seedlings each year; if you wish to share seedlings with friends, transplant while the plants are young and have only two to four leaves.

Spider Flower

This tall and airy annual, sometimes called cleome, shrugs off heat and drought and blooms from early summer until the first killing frost. By summer's end, each plant may stand 5 feet tall and sport a half dozen spreading stalks that wave in even the slightest breeze. Because of its tall stalks and large leaves, spider flower tends to dwarf its own airy blossoms of white, pink, or lavender. You can grow spider flower as an annual hedge or plant it at the rear of a mixed border. It also looks great in a carefree cottage garden or in front of a picket fence.

Spider flower is one of the best annuals for flower arrangements because of its unusual blooms with long stamens that resemble spider legs. The petals curl up during the hotter part of the day and then slowly unfurl in the cooler evening. The best time to cut new blossoms is in late afternoon and evening when spider flower springs to life. Its long, coiled stamens burst forth, popping open the day's new flowers.

Planting and Care

The easiest way to start spider flower is to sow seed directly in the garden in early spring, about two weeks before the last frost. Space the plants 3 feet apart. If planted too close together, plants become thin and scrawny. Because transplants will outgrow their tiny pots quickly, they are often hard to find in a nursery. If you should find them, wait until after the last frost to plant.

For best effect in the landscape, plant spider flower in large masses. Select a site in full sun with well-drained soil. Once established, spider flower tolerates dry weather, but the lower leaves turn yellow and the flowers wilt quickly if the plant needs water.

Starting from Seed

To grow your own transplants, start seed four to six weeks before the last frost. The seed should germinate in a couple of weeks if kept at a temperature of 65 to 70 degrees. Spider flower may be annual, but there is a saying about it: once you have it, you have it. This means that plants reseed and come up plentifully year after year. If you should want to prevent reseeding, simply cut off the seed pods before they mature and turn brown.

In the cool of late afternoon, spider flower pops open with fresh new blooms.

AT A GLANCE

❖

SPIDER FLOWER
Cleome hasslerana

Features: tall, dramatic, heat-tolerant plant

Colors: white, pink, lavender

Height: 3 to 5 feet

Light: full sun to light shade

Soil: well drained

Water: low

Pests: Japanese beetles

Remarks: easy, old-fashioned flower ideal for cottage gardens

This pure white selection mixes well with the typical spider flower, which is usually bicolored.

Different Selections

The common species found in old gardens features bicolored blossoms of lilac and white that fade in the heat. Newer selections come in solid colors and do not fade as quickly. Among them are White Queen, Rose Queen, Cherry Queen, Ruby Queen, Violet Queen, and Helen Campbell, a white selection.

Troubleshooting

Plants tend to grow straight up with few flowering stalks. You can prevent this by snipping a few inches off the top of each developing stalk before it blooms; two flowering stalks will replace it. Do this two or three times and by midsummer the plant will be covered in blossoms. If you remove the seed pods as they form, the plant will bloom until frost.

Japanese beetles sometimes eat both the flowers and the foliage. See page 235 for more about Japanese beetles.

Tall, white spider flowers—ringed by low-growing petunias—create a light, cloudlike effect in the midst of summer.

Sunflower

Once relegated to the backyard, sunflowers are now a proud annual in the most prominent beds. Sunflowers have been bred into shorter, more branched plants featuring a variety of broad blooms in yellow, orange, bronze, and even white and bicolored. Their pioneer stock makes them hardy, drought-tolerant plants deservedly popular for borders, as screens, or alone in a showy bed.

Small-flowered, branched selections make excellent cut flowers for a classic, country bouquet or as part of an elegant table setting. Those with a dark *corolla,* the ring around the center of the bloom, make especially lovely cut flowers. For an extra splash of color in the landscape, plant sunflowers with zinnias, another great annual for cutting. The traditional selections, with one giant bloom atop an 8-foot stalk, produce seeds for roasting or for feeding birds. Because of their impressive size, these mammoth types are great fun for children to grow.

Planting and Care

The best way to start sunflowers is to sow seed directly in the garden. Sow in spring after all danger of frost has passed, and choose a spot that gets full sun. Use the spacing recommended on the seed packet, especially for taller plants. If the plants get just a bit of shade from nearby trees in the morning or afternoon, they will grow even taller. Sunflowers do not require much fertilizer but do need water to keep their big leaves from wilting in dry weather. If you do not water, the

Small-flowered, branched selections make excellent cut flowers.

Sunflower seeds develop at the center of the bloom, turning from green to brown as they mature.

AT A GLANCE

❖

SUNFLOWER
Helianthus annuus

Features: tall summer annual with large blooms

Colors: white, yellow, orange, bronze, bicolored

Height: 15 inches to 10 feet

Light: full sun

Soil: average

Water: low to medium

Pests: none specific

Remarks: easy to grow from seed, great for attracting birds

Sunflower

Giant sunflowers always bloom facing the sun.

plants are not likely to die; however, the leaves may turn brown on the edges and disfigure a flowerbed.

Because mammoth types only produce one big flower, you may wish to stagger plantings a couple of weeks apart to enjoy fresh blooms for a longer period. Even with the smaller-flowered, branching types that produce more blooms as you cut, the initial planting may begin to look bedraggled by the end of summer. Replanting in early summer will give you a fresh crop that lasts through fall. At the end of the season, let the flowers ripen to seed so that you can collect them for next year, or let the seed drop to the ground to come up on its own next spring.

Large sunflowers produce striking flower heads, which can be as large as a dinner plate.

Stake tall sunflowers to keep them upright during rough weather.

Selections with a dark corolla are especially prized for arrangements.

Different Selections

Sunflowers have been hybridized into a variety of ornamental sizes and colors, including plants that branch and produce many flowers. Dwarf selections include Dwarf Sungold, which has double flowers and grows to 15 to 24 inches tall, and Sunspot, which has large 10-inch yellow flowers on plants that stand only 2 feet tall.

Medium-height selections are good for flower-beds and for cutting. They include Piccolo, which produces 4-foot-tall plants with bright yellow 4-inch flowers; Luna, known for branching plants with lots of pastel yellow blooms on stalks about 5 feet tall; and Italian White, prized for its 4-inch creamy flowers on plants about 4 feet tall. Large-flowered Mixed, which bears 6-inch flowers in yellow, orange, red, and bronze on bushy 5-foot plants, is an attractive selection for a bed, as is Sunbeam, a 5- to 7-foot plant prized for cutting because of its greenish, pollen-free center.

Among giant selections (8 to 10 feet tall) are Giganteus, Mammoth Russian, and Moonwalker. These are the classic, single-stalked selections that are topped with one giant bloom and used as accents in a garden. The seeds of these large selections are the biggest and the best for roasting.

Piccolo is a selection with lemon yellow blooms and a showy dark center. The more you cut it, the more flowers it will produce.

Sweet Alyssum

The fine texture of sweet alyssum combines with gerbera daisies for a striking contrast.

Sweet alyssum weaves a carpet of tiny flowers that bring a welcome honey fragrance to the early spring garden. A low-growing, spreading annual, sweet alyssum grows 6 to 12 inches wide but only 8 inches tall and flourishes in full sun while the weather is cool.

Because of its creeping growth habit, sweet alyssum makes an excellent choice for containers, edgings, or the front of a border. The plants sometimes flower so exuberantly that they hide their foliage, making a wonderful informal ground cover in a bed of bulbs, such as crocus and hyacinth, or in a rock garden. Plant it in front of sweet William or pansies, or at the base of shrubs. Sweet alyssum is also effective between stones in a pathway or rock wall, in hanging baskets and window boxes with cascading petunias or pansies, and anywhere you can use a blanket of fragrant flowers.

AT A GLANCE
❖
SWEET ALYSSUM
Lobularia maritima

Features: old-fashioned, fragrant mat of blooms in early spring

Colors: white, lavender, rose, purple

Height: 3 to 8 inches

Light: full sun

Soil: well drained

Water: medium to high

Pests: none specific

Remarks: attractive in pots and window boxes

Planting and Care

Start sweet alyssum from seed or transplants. Because this is a cool-weather annual, it is important to sow seed in the garden early, four to six weeks before the last frost. Do not cover them; just sprinkle the seed on top of moist soil in full sun or very light shade. The tiny seeds are easier to spread if you mix them with sand and rake them into the soil very lightly. Transplants set out in early spring can tolerate light frost.

Sweet alyssum begins to bloom five to six weeks after seeding. It blooms for several months if kept trimmed; otherwise, the blooms go to seed. Keep the soil moist, but do not overwater.

Sweet alyssum enjoys cool, sunny weather. When temperatures rise, sweet alyssum declines. However, if given plenty of water, it survives in areas with cool summers and blooms again. You can pull up the old plants and sow new seed in late summer for a fresh crop in fall. Plants allowed to produce seed will reseed, and seedlings will reappear again the following spring.

Different Selections

Popular white selections range from 4 to 6 inches high and include Carpet of Snow, Tiny Tim, and Snow Crystals. Wonderland is a series of 4-inch-tall plants that come in a choice of rose, white, and purple. Violet Queen is prized for its rich violet flowers. Rosie O'Day, an All-America Selections winner, has rosy blooms on 3-inch plants. All selections of sweet alyssum are quite fragrant.

Sow sweet alyssum between paving stones for a sweet-smelling carpet in early spring.

Mix sweet alyssum with petunias in a pot and place in a sunny location.

Sweet Pea

Climbing sweet peas are vinelike annuals that need a fence or trellis on which to climb.

AT A GLANCE
❖
SWEET PEA
Lathyrus odoratus

Features: colorful, fragrant spring vine or bush

Colors: red, purple, lilac, white, pink, blue

Height: 9 inches to 8 feet

Light: full sun to light shade

Soil: moist, fertile, neutral to slightly alkaline

Water: medium to high

Pests: aphids, slugs, spider mites

Remarks: does not like hot weather

The appeal of this charming annual, which thrives in cool weather, is its fluffy, translucent blooms that spring from slender stems. Sweet peas may be one of many colors—red, deep purple, lilac, white, pale pink, or blue—and always enliven their surroundings with a distinctive honey-orange scent.

There are two forms of sweet peas that may be easily grown from seed. Bush or dwarf types, which grow about 2½ feet tall, are good for beds, borders, and containers. Plant these sweet peas near spring bulbs so that they may hide the fading foliage of bulbs. Climbing types, which can grow up to 8 feet in length, make charming accent vines and screens. These easily climb fences, gateposts, and other vertical structures. Both types provide delightful blooms for cutting to bring indoors.

Planting and Care

Sow sweet pea seeds in the fall in the Lower and Coastal South. Sow in early spring in cooler climates, as soon as the ground can be worked. Good timing is essential; sweet pea does not like hot weather and needs to be established and blooming before summer's heat begins. In areas where you can plant in fall, it will overwinter, even if the tops of the plants appear to die. Growth resumes vigorously from the roots in spring. You can also start sweet peas indoors six weeks before transplanting outdoors.

Sweet pea likes full sun to light shade and rich, moist soil. If your soil is acid, bring the pH up to 7.0 by adding lime. Prepare a rich bed by digging a trench 1 foot deep and equally wide; fill it with organic matter before sowing seed.

Soak the large seeds for several hours before planting. They absorb water faster if you nick their surfaces with a nail file. Plant seeds 6 inches apart, poking them about ½ inch into the soil. When seedlings appear, mulch them to keep the roots cool. Water regularly and deadhead old blooms to ensure that the plant continues to flower until the weather gets hot.

Both types of sweet pea have very thin stems that need support. Plants grab their supports with thin, curly tendrils, like those of edible peas. Always use thin twig, wire, or string supports, because the tendrils cannot wrap around thick props. Stake climbing types with a bean trellis, chicken wire, bamboo canes or twigs arranged in a tepee, or a wire fence. Dwarf selections do not need much support; simply prop them up with twigs.

Different Selections

Many gardeners prefer older selections that are quite heat tolerant, like the first wild sweet pea believed to have originated in Italy. Pink Perfume, a 15-inch bush type, produces pale pink flowers and a pleasing fragrance. Also available in an array of colors are Patio Mixed, an early-blooming 9-inch bush and Bijou, an early-blooming 10- to 12-inch bush. Any of these would work well in a window box, in a pot, or as an edging plant.

Supersnoop, which grows to about 2½ feet tall, blooms early, making it a good choice for places where spring warms up quickly. Old Spice is a collection of old-fashioned, fragrant climbing selections from Sicily. Royal Family Mixed is a fine climbing sweet pea, with large flowers and some resistance to heat. Galaxy Mixed is another climber that boasts long, strong stems with five or more large flowers.

Troubleshooting

Sweet peas are frequently bothered by aphids, slugs, and spider mites. Turn to pages 234 and 236 for more about these pests.

The butterfly-like blossoms of sweet peas are so named for their sweet fragrance.

Sweet William

This dwarf selection of mixed colors stays very compact, making it an ideal choice for the edge of a garden.

Sweet William has been a fragrant part of American gardens since colonial days. When planted liberally, its light scent in early spring perfumes the garden and invites butterflies. When cut, its blooms are a delightful addition to an arrangement of cut flowers.

Often planted in fall to bloom the next spring, sweet William is a dependable and showy annual for the cool months of spring. Its large clusters of fragrant flowers also make sweet William a nice choice for pots near the terrace or deck. Indoors, one or two cut stems practically make a whole bouquet.

Planting and Care

Sweet William may behave like a biennial. If planted in the spring, it grows throughout the summer to become a thick clump of foliage, about 18 inches across. The plentiful leaves help keep the garden green through winter. In the mild winters of the South, the foliage withstands freezing. It may droop overnight during extreme cold, but it will perk up as the day warms. (Although biennial, some selections have been so improved by breeding that they bloom the first spring if planted early.)

Start plants from seed or transplants. Plant in rich, organic soil in full sun (with afternoon shade) and good drainage. If your garden has acid soil, sprinkle 1 cup of lime for every 10 square feet before planting. In the South, set out transplants or sow seed directly in the garden in fall for spring color; farther north, sow in early

Flowers of sweet William are clustered into showy balls that brighten a spring border.

spring for summer flowers. Sweet William often reseeds itself, providing year after year of fragrant blossoms. You can also collect seeds or dig young seedlings to transplant in the spring.

Cutting spent flowers before they produce seed keeps plants blooming longer, but the flowers must remain on the plant to reseed.

Different Selections

Sweet William has changed very little over time. It blooms in white, purples, pinks, and crimson, the same as it has for years. Dwarf types are also available. (See page 188 for information on other *Dianthus species.*)

Selections include Pride of Park Avenue, with graceful 18- to 24-inch stems that carry brightly colored blooms and are tall enough to stand in a vase. Indian Carpet is a dwarf selection that grows into a ruglike ground cover of 8-inch tall flowering stalks. Wee Willie is even more compact (3 to 6 inches) and is good for edging, with single blooms available in a mixture of colors.

Sweet William will perfume an entire garden in spring.

Wax Begonia

The glossy green leaves of Victory White wax begonias make the blossoms appear even whiter.

Cool and crisp on even the hottest of days, wax begonia creates a steady show of color from early spring until frost. The offspring of plants native to Brazil, today's hybrids boast upturned, succulent green or bronze leaves and ground-hugging clouds of small silky flowers. The blooms, in elegant reds, creamy whites, and sedate pinks, add reliable color to any area of your garden. In rain or shine, sun or shade, begonias work well in flowerbeds and borders, as well as window boxes and other containers.

Wax begonias are most attractive in the garden when planted in gently curving lines. Ranging from 6 to 18 inches tall, they also make excellent edging plants for walkways and the borders of raised beds. Small groupings of three to five plants can serve as spots of color in a shaded or partially sunny border. Wax begonias are also naturals for pots and window boxes because they are heat-hardy and their delicate flowers can be best appreciated when viewed up close. Combine green-leafed selections with ferns, coleus, or caladiums to create a refreshing niche in the shade. Bronze-leafed selections make comely companions for silver plants, such as annual dusty miller or perennial artemisia.

Planting and Care

Set out transplants after all danger of frost has passed. Plant in rich soil that retains moisture but drains well. If you have poor drainage, amend the soil with compost and other organic material, or add extra soil to raise the beds. Wax begonias do well under hot, humid conditions, although they may bloom less profusely during the sultry days of August. During that time, you will appreciate the color and texture of their leaves as much as their blooms.

Wax begonias are drought tolerant once established, but do not let new transplants dry out. In the absence of rain, water once a week. However, be careful with container plants; their roots are likely to rot, so do not overwater. Allow the top layer, about 1 inch of soil, to dry between waterings. If container plants start to look leggy in late summer, pinch dead flowers and unwieldy sprouts.

Wax begonias need extra fertilizer in midsummer; apply a controlled-release flower food. (See page 43 to read about fertilizers.) If your begonias look tired by September, consider replacing them with a new set of transplants, which will be in the garden centers for fall.

Wax begonias make excellent edging plants, providing a tidy contrast to the surrounding landscape.

Different Selections

Green-leafed selections are well suited for shade, while the bronze-leafed selections take more sun. For partial or morning sun locations, the best series is the bronze-leafed Cocktail Series, which grows from 6 to 8 inches tall. Selections include Gin, with deep pink flowers, Vodka, with red flowers, Brandy, with light pink flowers, and Whiskey, with white flowers.

Among green-leafed wax begonias is the tried-and-true Olympia series, which includes blooms in white, pink, red, salmon, and starlet (white with rosy red margins). The Encore series includes both bronze- and green-leafed selections, such as the lovely Encore White/Bronze, with dramatic dark leaves. Encore begonias grow about a foot tall and are a bit more floppy than other selections, resulting in a looser appearance than the more tightly mounded types.

Wax begonias can handle the occasional dry conditions of a container; their mounding habit is perfect for those that are bowl-shaped.

Zinnia

With flowers held high on sturdy stems, tall zinnias are prized for both flowerbeds and cutting gardens.

Zinnias are hard to beat for spectacular color and dependable blooms from summer through fall. Their brilliant color makes them a yearly favorite for the seasoned gardener, and their ease and dependability make them perfect for the inexperienced, too. Zinnias are ideal cut flowers; no other annual offers as many colorful blooms for cutting. The cut flowers last about a week and do not shed their leaves when they die; they simply fade and then turn brown.

Zinnias come in a full range of plant heights and flower sizes suited for flowerbeds and cutting gardens. Plant them in a solid mass of one color, set out a few plants as summer filler in a perennial border, use low plants for edging and containers, or mix all the colors together in a bed or border for a fiesta of flowers. They are also excellent plants for a child's garden because they do well in summer, sprout quickly, attract butterflies, and bloom in so many bright colors.

Planting and Care

Start zinnias from seed or from purchased transplants. The seeds are large and easy to sow; plant at least two weeks after the last frost. In the South, you can sow zinnias as late as July for color in late summer and early fall. Choose a sunny location with well-drained soil. Zinnias are not fussy about soil but bloom best in rich, moist ground, such as that of a vegetable garden. In fact, vegetable gardeners sometimes plant a row of zinnias in the garden to attract bees for pollination. Water zinnias regularly until they are established; although forgiving in dry weather, they bloom more and the foliage is healthier if they are well watered during periods of drought. Keep zinnias blooming furiously by fertilizing every six weeks with a controlled-release flower food and by cutting spent blooms so that the plants will produce more.

The more you cut zinnias, the more they bloom. If left uncut, they go to seed, stop blooming, and die. If you want long, unbranched stems for cutting, remove side branches as the plant grows. This technique will also give you the largest flowers. Plants growing 24 inches and taller should be staked, especially in areas prone to summer thunderstorms.

AT A GLANCE
❖
ZINNIA
Zinnia elegans

Features: brilliant colors from summer to frost, good for cutting

Colors: white, orange, pink, red, yellow, lavender

Height: 6 to 36 inches

Light: full sun

Soil: well drained, fertile

Water: low to medium

Pests: powdery mildew

Remarks: quick flowering, good for beginners

Different Selections

Zinnias come in two flower shapes. Those with flat-petaled blooms are known as dahlia-flowered and have a perfect geometric fullness. They include the California Giants and Giant Sun Hybrids, an All-America Selections winner. Cactus-flowered zinnias have petals that curl along the sides, giving the blossom a feathery, irregular outline. Among these are All-America Selections winners Wild Cherry, Carved Ivory, and the more mildew-resistant Zenith Hybrids; also available are Rosy Future, Torch, Firecracker, and Yellow Zenith.

Zinnia plants come in four sizes, lending them to many uses in the garden. Extra dwarf plants bloom the earliest and include the Thumbelina and Mini series. Plants are about 6 inches tall with a mounded form, making them good for borders and containers. Dwarfs grow from 7 to 14 inches tall. This group includes the Pinwheel series, which have small single flowers and creep like a ground cover rather than growing upright like other selections. Other dwarfs, such as the Peter Pan series, an All-America Selections winner, have large flowers atop small plants and appear to be shrunken versions of taller types. They may be used for colorful impact at the front of a border, for mass plantings, and in containers.

Zinnias offer long-lasting cut flowers in an assortment of brilliant colors.

Narrow-leaf zinnia creeps like a ground cover, softening a walkway with mounds of flowers.

The half-tall category includes the Lilliput series and the mildew-resistant Sun series; both grow from 18 to 24 inches tall and are popular for cutting. Tall ones reach a height of 24 to 36 inches. These include the Ruffles Hybrids, known for ruffled double blooms that are 2 to 4 inches wide and are popular for borders and cottage gardens as well as for cutting. The Zenith hybrids have blooms up to 6 inches wide and are spectacular for cutting.

Dahlia-flowered zinnias have flat petals and are perfectly symmetrical in form.

The curved petals of this cactus-flowered zinnia give the bloom a ruffled look.

AT A GLANCE

❖

NARROW-LEAF ZINNIA
Zinnia angustifolia

Features: very heat tolerant, nonstop blooms until frost

Colors: orange, creamy white

Height: 12 inches

Light: full sun

Soil: well drained

Water: low to medium

Pests: powdery mildew

Remarks: looks like a wildflower

Narrow-leaf Zinnia

Narrow-leaf zinnia *(Zinnia angustifolia),* which is a different species from the standard garden zinnia, has the look of a wildflower. A dependable, heat-tolerant annual, it blooms from spring until frost and is covered with daisylike flowers in orange or white. It grows into a multibranched, creeping plant about 12 inches tall and twice as wide with slender, blue-green leaves. Because of its growth habit, this zinnia is popular for massing like a ground cover or planting where it can spill over a wall or the edge of a container. Its loose, wildflower-like habit also makes narrow-leaf zinnia suitable for sunny areas of a natural, informal landscape. You may sometimes see it sold as *Zinnia linearis,* its former scientific name.

Start narrow-leaf zinnia from seed or from transplants; it needs the same conditions and care as other zinnias.

Troubleshooting

In humid climates, zinnias are prone to powdery mildew, a fungus that looks like white mildew on the foliage and causes the leaves to wither. Avoid watering with overhead sprinklers; use a soaker hose instead and water in early morning so plants have time to dry. Adequate spacing between plants will also provide good air circulation so that the leaves can dry quickly after a rain. The best way to avoid powdery mildew is to plant mildew-resistant selections, such as the Zenith hybrids. Turn to page 235 to read more about powdery mildew.

Be prepared to support tall zinnias with thin stakes or grow-through plant supports. Their flowers are often so big and heavy that even the sturdiest stems are bent by rain.

Pink and yellow zinnias are the focal point of this summer bed at Callaway Gardens in Pine Mountain, Georgia.

Plant Hardiness Zone Map

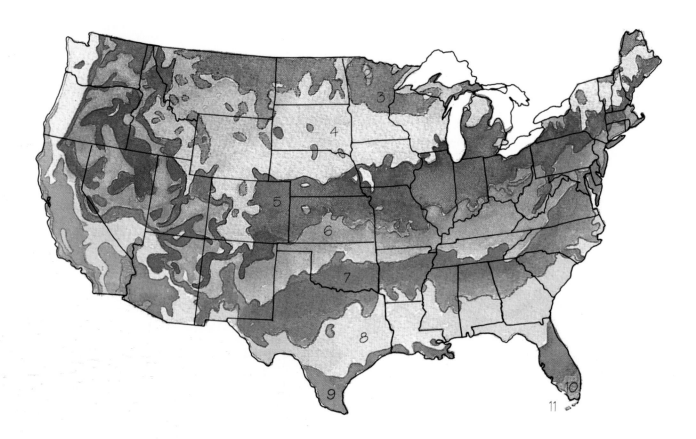

The United States Department of Agriculture (USDA) has charted low temperatures throughout the country to determine the ranges of average low readings. The map above is based loosely on the USDA Plant Hardiness Zone Map, which was drawn from these findings. It does not take into account heat, soil, or moisture extremes and is intended as a guide, not a guarantee.

The southern regions of the United States that are mentioned in this book refer to the following:

Upper South: Zone 6

Middle South: upper region of Zone 7 (0 to 5 degrees minimum)

Lower South: lower region of Zone 7 and upper region of Zone 8 (5 to 15 degrees minimum)

Coastal South: lower region of Zone 8 and upper region of Zone 9 (15 to 25 degrees minimum)

Tropical South: lower region of Zone 9 and all of Zone 10 (25 to 40 degrees minimum)

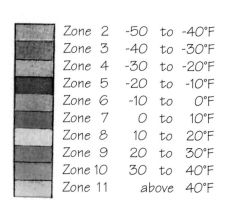

Zone 2	-50 to -40°F
Zone 3	-40 to -30°F
Zone 4	-30 to -20°F
Zone 5	-20 to -10°F
Zone 6	-10 to 0°F
Zone 7	0 to 10°F
Zone 8	10 to 20°F
Zone 9	20 to 30°F
Zone 10	30 to 40°F
Zone 11	above 40°F

Perennial Profiles

Coneflowers and salvia

The perennials described in the following pages were selected by the garden editors at *Southern Living* on the basis of their beauty, adaptability, and value in the garden. They represent a wide spectrum of perennials, from those that thrive anywhere—in full sun and sandy soil—to those that need rich soil and regular attention. Many are tried-and-true favorites that have worked for gardeners for years.

Like the Annual Profiles, the Perennial Profiles are arranged alphabetically by common name. Each profile has a description of the plant, information about planting and propagating, and suggested ways to incorporate its color, height, and form into your garden, along with companion plantings.

You'll also find information on the soil and cultural conditions a plant needs to thrive, tips for keeping the plant looking its best, and troubleshooting solutions to help you fight pests and diseases.

When a genus contains more than one related species, as coreopsis does, the group is combined in a single entry. The profile points out the differences in appearance and growing needs of the most popular species and hybrids.

For a quick overview of the plant, refer to the *At a Glance* box that accompanies every profile. This lists the major features of the perennial, such as its soil and light requirements. The box also includes the plant's botanical name to help you avoid confusion when buying perennials.

Try experimenting with new perennials in your garden each year. Feel free to plant those that you have never grown before or that are only marginally suited to your climate.

You will find a natural variation among plants growing under different conditions. For example, flower colors are brighter in cool, crisp weather; plants often stretch taller in shade than they would grow in sun; and most are shorter in hot, dry climates. All this is a normal part of plant response, so keep it in mind when local information is different from what you see or read here.

Artemisia

The silver leaves of artemisia make vivid flowers such as orange marigolds and yellow threadleaf coreopsis appear even brighter.

Prized for the soft gray or silvery color of its leaves, artemisia seems to exist to make other plants look good. Its foliage offers an easy way to spotlight the flower or foliage colors of adjacent plants; it also adds an unusual silvery component to flower beds, borders, and containers. Most selections have leaves that are fragrant when brushed against or crushed, and all are useful in arrangements.

In the Landscape

Most of your garden plants will look better in the company of artemisias. Good companions are flowers that trail, such as verbena or narrow-leaf zinnia, because they tend to wind through the artemisia's silver leaves. For cool effects, try plants that bloom blue or pink, such as forget-me-nots and sweet William. Other good partners are hardy salvias, Autumn Joy sedum, and any type of dianthus. You can always use artemisia throughout a planting to unify a bed of varied colors.

Planting and Care

Artemisias grow best in full sun, although a few hours of afternoon shade helps them stand up to hot Southern summers. Plants sometimes struggle in the heat and humidity of the Lower South, especially in rainy summers when the foliage stays wet. Some selections such as Valerie Finnis and Powis Castle seem a bit more tolerant of the summer conditions than do the popular Silver King and Silver Mound. In the Middle and Upper South, most artemisias do well. Plants need good air circulation and a well-drained spot that dries out between waterings.

Set out transplants in spring or fall, in well-drained, cultivated soil. Pinch off the growing tip of large transplants so that the plants will develop bushy branches. After a year or two, plants often become woody; cut them back to 6 or 8 inches to encourage fresh new growth. You can also dig up and divide old plants in spring

---

AT A GLANCE

❖

ARTEMISIA
Artemisia species

Features: shimmering foliage

Colors: silvery gray, gray green

Height: 10 to 36 inches

Light: full sun

Soil: well drained

Water: low

Pests: none specific

Native: no

Range: Zones 4 to 9

Remarks: combines well with any color

---

or fall. Stem cuttings taken in spring rapidly develop roots when set in containers filled with damp potting soil.

Silver King often spreads by underground runners, which you can dig and replant elsewhere.

Different Selections

Some artemisias form mounds less than 1 foot tall, but the better ones for the South, Powis Castle and Valerie Finnis, grow upright to about 3 feet tall and equally wide. Some species of artemisia produce small yellow flowers, but they aren't particularly showy. Many gardeners prefer to pinch the flowers off as they appear. Try using nonflowering, compact varieties, such as Silver Brocade, as edgings or accent plants for the front of the border.

Look for artemisias that grow to the size and form you want for a certain spot. Silver Mound and Silver King are two of the most common selections with very silvery leaves. Feathery Powis Castle grows into a broad mound of light textured gray green foliage. Valerie Finnis is a stronger silver gray. Silver Brocade, one of the prettiest artemisias, has dainty scalloped leaves that resemble silvery gray lace; its leaves are so bright that they appear nearly white.

Silver Mound artemisia lines a walk also bordered by lamb's ears, purple larkspur, Shasta daisies, and pink geraniums.

Arum

After arum's leaves die back in late spring, red berries appear on the old flower stalks.

Arum looks like a small tropical plant, but it is at its peak during the coldest time of year. Few perennials are more intriguing in both looks and behavior. Not only does arum's foliage pop through the soil in fall, a time when most things are about to die back, but the unusual leaves also endure freeze after freeze until warm weather arrives.

In late fall, green-and-white arrow-shaped leaves emerge, each almost a foot long and as rippled and exotic as crocodile skin. The foliage is hardy in all regions of the South. Even if very cold weather appears to have damaged the plant, the leaves will sprout anew. But most gardeners can count on its interesting presence all winter long.

In spring, pale green callalike flowers appear, reminiscent of jack-in-the-pulpit. In late spring, the leaves die back as the plant goes dormant. Then, in early summer, a short stalk of glossy red berries may appear on two- to three-year-old plants that receive bright light.

In the Landscape

Use arum under trees and in other shady spots. It is quite tolerant of deep shade and makes a nice winter blanket in the shade. Beautify the winter garden by planting arum in groups on the north side of your house for a focal point along a walkway or a patio. It is also a hard-working winter ground cover that contrasts handsomely with other evergreens or plants with winter interest, such as Lenten rose and evergreen ferns. If planted in a moist, shady location, arum will slowly spread to become a handsome ground cover.

Combine arum with hostas for year-round ground cover. The hostas will cover the ground from spring into summer while the arum is dormant. Caladiums are another good summer companion, but be careful not to damage arum's roots when planting caladium tubers.

Different Selections

Although few named selections are commonly found, one called Pictum has particularly striking silver markings on the foliage and is a bit more variegated than the white-veined species.

The exotic-looking leaves of arum are unexpected from a cold-hardy winter perennial.

Planting and Care

Plant arum in partial shade in moist, rich soil. If you let the seeds ripen and fall to the ground, they will be the source of new seedlings that you can share with friends. You can divide the plant in fall by separating the clumps of leaves as they break through the ground. Dig carefully and deeply. The fleshy foliage is easily broken away from the roots, which can make the bulbous root becomes nearly impossible to find.

Aster

Daisylike blooms with yellow centers characterize all asters. This selection is Harrington's Pink.

Because of their hardy nature and royal autumn show, asters are on the "must have" list of many veteran gardeners, and rightly so. Just when summer has taken its toll on much of the garden, asters begin to bloom—quietly at first, opening only a few blossoms, and then showering the garden with daisylike flowers in white, blue, purple, lavender, pink, and even yellow. As the nights get cooler in September and October, the colors of the flowers intensify.

In the Landscape

Asters vary from 6 inches to 7 feet tall, allowing for many uses in the garden. Taller asters are perfect for late summer and fall color at the back of a flower border, while dwarf selections can edge a border or even comprise a mass planting. Asters are also popular used singly sprinkled through a rock garden. Often purchased in full bloom, asters create instant color in containers or window boxes and can be transplanted to the garden after the blooms fade.

Asters can certainly stand by themselves, but their beauty is perhaps most fully realized when they are combined with other fall-blooming perennials. Grow them alongside goldenrod, Formosa lily, and blue or purple salvias. Other useful late-blooming companions include ornamental grasses, mums, boltonia, and Mexican mint marigold. Many selections also make excellent cut flowers.

Tatarian aster grows to 7 feet and works well at the back of a fall flower border.

AT A GLANCE
❖
ASTER
Aster species

Features: fall flowers with a rich variety of colors

Colors: blue, purple, lavender, red, pink, white, yellow

Height: 6 inches to 7 feet

Light: full sun

Soil: well drained

Water: medium

Pests: powdery mildew

Native: some

Range: Zones 5 to 8

Remarks: a plant with many landscape uses

Species and Selections

Open any catalog and you will see at least a half-dozen different improved selections. New aster cultivars are introduced every year, so shop around for different colors, heights, and foliage. Often they are selections of one of the following major types.

New England aster *(Aster novae-angliae)* is also native to the South, despite its name. Selections range from 3 to 5 feet in height. While most bloom in some shade of purple, New England asters may also be red or pink. Most bloom in September and October, but Harrington's Pink and Alma Potschke (deep rose) begin blooming in midsummer with flowers that are 2 inches across. Autumn Snow is a late-blooming white, a rare color among this group of asters.

New York aster *(Aster novi-belgii),* also called Michaelmas daisy, is the parent plant of many hybrid asters. This species is also a Southern native and typically grows 3 to 4 feet tall with blue-violet blooms. Hybrids feature single, semidouble, or double flowers of white, lavender, pink, blue, rose, purple, or red. Heights range from the 10 or 12 inches of the selection Professor Anton Kippenburg to the 4 feet of Coombe Violet. Most selections bloom in September and October, but some bloom earlier. As cut flowers they are superior to New England asters, which close soon after cutting.

Skydrop aster *(Aster patens),* another native, deserves much wider use. It grows 2 to 3 feet tall and bears bright violet-blue flowers on delicate, upright stems. Like all true asters, its blossoms sport yellow centers. It is very late blooming and quite tolerant of dry fall weather.

Aromatic aster *(Aster oblongifolius)* grows to a bushy mound about 2 feet high. Lavender flowers appear atop leaves that are pleasantly fragrant when crushed. This native plant is durable, drought tolerant, and trouble free, and it is among the latest asters to bloom, usually in November.

Tatarian aster *(Aster tataricus)* adds impact to the garden with leaves that may be 2 feet long and with spikes of pale blue-purple flowers that top 7-foot stems. It blooms late, often into November, and although it is not a native plant, it is very dependable and thrives in sandy or heavy soils. Tatarian aster is striking when massed at the back of the border; pair it with tall ornamental grasses for a lovely natural look. It needs a sturdy stake to keep it from falling over. Jindai is a lower-growing selection that matures at only 4 feet tall and is less likely to need staking than other asters.

Many selections of the dependable New England asters exist, ranging from 3 to 5 feet.

Weighted by rain, the lanky stems of tatarian aster rest on Autumn Joy sedum.

Golden aster departs from the usual pink and lavender to sport blooms of rich yellow in late summer and early autumn.

Golden aster *(Aster linosyris)* is a bright, cheery aster that grows 18 to 20 inches tall and bears yellow blooms in late summer and early fall.

Frikart aster *(Aster* x *frikartii)* is a mildew-resistant, long-blooming plant that bears its lavender flowers much earlier than other asters, typically in early to midsummer, and continues to bloom for weeks if you remove the dead flowers. In the Lower and Coastal South it generally behaves as an annual.

Planting and Care

Asters prefer full sun but will tolerate light shade. Some grow well in dry soil, but most like consistent moisture. Good drainage is essential. These perennials do well throughout the South except near the coast, where summer heat and humidity may cause the plants to rot. The height of tall asters can be a problem in small gardens. To keep these plants a manageable size, cut them back by 6 inches in the spring and in midsummer. You will have shorter, stockier plants that bloom in the fall and should not need to be staked.

Divide plants every two to three years to keep them vigorous. Divide in early spring or fall, lifting each clump and separating the youngest asters to replant; discard the old center.

Troubleshooting

Powdery mildew plagues the foliage of many asters in spring and fall. See page 235 for more about powdery mildew.

Dwarf asters are perfect for a rock garden, an edging, or the front of a border.

Astilbe

Deep pink is one of the more popular shades of astilbe.

Gardeners who grow astilbe treasure the ephemeral beauty and stunning color it brings to the summer shade garden. And despite rumors that it is finicky, astilbe performs well in the South.

Several species of astilbe, which is native to China and Japan, thrive in shade in the South. Their feathery pink, peach, red, or white plumes soften and decorate the landscape like icing on a cake. In the southern limit of astilbe's range, the feathery flower spikes appear in midspring, while farther north they usually wait until summer. Flowers appear from mid-May through August, but astilbe's fernlike foliage—ranging from deep green to copper—exudes a quiet elegance for months on end.

In the Landscape

Plants range from 1 to 4 feet in height, with shorter selections for the front of the garden and taller plants for the back of the border. Staking is not needed. Plant a mass of astilbe in a shady bed to create a summer focal point, or plant three in the corner of a shady border for a colorful accent. Since astilbe enjoys moist soil, it is great for grouping near birdbaths, ponds, and other water features.

Try astilbes in large sweeps for dramatic effect, or plant them in a perennial border with other plants that need similar growing conditions. Combine them with hostas, goldenray, Japanese anemones, stokesia, and dead nettle, all of which bring color and texture to shade.

Astilbe works well with hostas in a perennial border; both plants prefer shade and moist, well-drained soil.

AT A GLANCE
❖
ASTILBE
Astilbe species and hybrids

Features: colorful summer plumes, fine-textured foliage for shade

Colors: pink, red, peach, creamy white, lavender

Height: 1 to 4 feet

Light: filtered morning sun or afternoon shade

Soil: moist, well drained

Water: high

Pests: none specific

Native: no

Range: Zones 4 to 8

Remarks: bears excellent flowers for cutting and nice foliage when not in bloom

The soft white blooms of this astilbe fall gracefully into a path as they reach for light.

Plant astilbes where they may be easily observed; their flowers have such richness and intricacy of detail that they merit close observation. They make excellent cut flowers if the blooms are harvested just after they open. Left on the plant, the flower spikes remain ornamental, even after blooming has ceased. And after the foliage and flowers die down, the seed heads that appear are also attractive, making astilbe a plant of many seasons.

Species and Selections

Astilbe *(Astilbe* x *arendsii)* is the most common group of hybrids. These plants bloom for at least three weeks and grow 1 to 4 feet tall, depending on the selection. Selections include Deutschland, which blooms in white; Fanal, which boasts deep red blooms; and Rheinland, which bears pink blooms. These selections mature at 2 feet tall. Red Sentinel is a 3-foot plant that blooms in bright red; Purple Blaze is a 4-foot plant with purple blooms.

Peach Blossom *(Astilbe* x *rosea* Peach Blossom*)* is a vigorous, 3- to 4-foot-tall hybrid that features showy salmon pink flowers in midspring.

Chinese astilbe *(Astilbe chinensis)* is a late-blooming species that will make a handsome ground cover as it spreads by underground stems. Pumila is a selection that grows 1 to 1½ feet tall; it has lavender-pink flower spikes that are dusted with a bluish silver hue.

Fall astilbe *(Astilbe taquetii)* is a rather tall species (up to 4 feet) that bears purple flowers in mid- to late summer. These blooms are especially nice for cutting. Fall astilbe is better adapted to the warm weather of the Lower and Coastal South than other species.

Planting and Care

Astilbes flourish throughout the South, except in the hottest parts. If you live in the Lower or Coastal South, you can grow astilbes, although the plants will not be as vigorous as they are in areas where they can get a longer winter rest. In fact, they may only live a year or two unless planted in a cool spot with plenty of moisture.

These perennials prefer deep, rich soil. Steady moisture is a must, particularly in summer. For that reason, plant astilbes in areas that can be watered in times of drought, and do not allow soil to dry out. They are not bog plants, however. They like water only when they are actively growing. If the soil is wet in winter, astilbes will rot.

Plant astilbes in either strong, filtered light or morning sun and afternoon shade. The farther south you live, the more shade astilbes require, though it should never be dense. These plants are heavy feeders and respond well to spring applications of controlled-release flower food.

Every three years or so, dig up the plants, divide them, and replant. Not only does this give you more plants, but it keeps them vigorous and blooming freely. Astilbe is a long-lived perennial when provided good conditions.

Long-lived and dependable, astilbe is a staple of flower borders.

The tall flower spikes of Fanal draw attention to any shady location. The flowers remain attractive even after they fade.

Begonia

Hardy begonia's unusual blooms bring a soft shade of pink to the garden in late summer and fall.

One of the most surprising perennials for the Southern garden in late summer and fall is hardy begonia. Most gardeners do not expect a begonia to be perennial because the most common ones are annual. However, this antique plant comes back faithfully and reseeds year after year in Zones 7 and 8, the warmer part of its range.

With its tropical-looking leaves and tubular flamingo-colored blooms, hardy begonia fills in shaded corners of the garden and attracts pleasant inquiries from passersby not familiar with its old-fashioned charm.

At a Glance

❖

HARDY BEGONIA
Begonia grandis

Features: colorful, heart-shaped leaves; late summer flowers

Colors: pink

Height: 1 to 2 feet

Light: partial shade

Soil: rich, light, well drained

Water: medium

Pests: none specific

Native: no

Range: Zones 6 to 8

Remarks: nice texture for shade, even when not in bloom

In the Landscape

Shade is a must for hardy begonia, which grows from 1 to 2 feet tall and has a loose, mounding form built on arching, fleshy stems. Its 3- to 6-inch light green leaves have red undersides, making hardy begonia interesting when planted at the edge of a wall or other place where the underside of the plant can be seen. Its texture is coarse and contrasts well with the finer leaves of other shade-loving plants, such as astilbes or ferns.

Hardy begonia also blends well in a naturalistic planting with Lenten rose and hosta. You can even use it as a seasonal ground cover under trees, interspersed with Italian arum or daffodils to take its place in winter when the foliage has died down. It also pairs well with tropical plants such as impatiens and ginger lily. Hardy begonia is an attractive plant for the front of the border; its heart-shaped leaves will gently arch over walkway edges. Because it spreads by reseeding, hardy begonia is a good choice for untended areas where the plants are able to spread as they may.

Different Selections

Most often sold only as hardy begonia, few named selections or hybrids of the plant are available.

Planting and Care

Hardy begonia needs rich soil with good drainage and must have protection from the hot midday and afternoon sun. Hardy begonias will flourish for years, even decades, if planted in the right location. They thrive in Zones 7 and 8, where winter is not too cold but is cool enough to provide the necessary period of dormancy. In Zone 6, plant them in a protected spot or mulch with pine straw or bark to protect tubers from the cold. Farther north, dig up hardy begonias in the fall and replant in the late spring, after the threat of frost is past.

You can dig plants when they first come up in spring to give away or to transplant to other parts of the garden. However, hardy begonia does not require dividing to keep it vigorous as do many other perennials. It reproduces by seed and tiny bulbs that form on the leaves; seedlings often need more than one year to bloom.

Hardy begonia fills shady corners with its lush foliage and colorful blooms.

Bleeding Heart

White bleeding heart brings light to a dark woodland floor.

Gardeners prize bleeding heart for its delicate blooms that dangle like bracelet charms in spring. The first part of its name is derived from the inner petals that "drip" from the tip of the heart-shaped outer petals and resemble a drop of blood (albeit white). The arching flower stems held above the foliage provide a charming companion to other shade-loving spring flowers, such as blue forget-me-nots. Two of the most popular species of bleeding heart are common bleeding heart, whose foliage dies down soon after the plant blooms, and fringed bleeding heart, a native whose foliage remains all summer.

In the Landscape

Because it is sure to be a conversation piece, place bleeding heart in a spot where it will be seen. Plant common bleeding heart in combination with compatible plants, such as ferns and hostas, that will fill the void when it disappears. Its wildflower-like qualities make it an excellent choice for wooded gardens in combination with daffodils, ferns, woodland phlox, hostas, and other shade-loving perennials.

Common bleeding heart forms a clump of loose, open, parsleylike foliage that is often floppy; for that reason, it looks best when planted in groups of three or more for a fuller look. However, fringed bleeding heart has fuller foliage and stiffer stems, so the plant does not flop. In fact, fringed bleeding heart keeps its foliage until fall if you do not let it dry out in summer.

Species and Selections

Common bleeding heart was introduced to America from Japan more than 100 years ago and has become a garden classic. This long-lived perennial is well adapted to growing conditions throughout the South, except the arid regions of Texas and south Florida. In early spring, the plants send up soft, bright green leaves. Later the flowering begins, with rose or white blossoms gradually unfolding from bottom to top along long arching racemes. After the flowers fall, the foliage turns yellow and gradually disappears; by midsummer, the plant is completely gone until the next year, which is why it is best to pair it with longer-lasting plants.

A surprising selection of common bleeding heart is the pure white Pantaloons, which grows larger and blooms more profusely than another popular white selection, Alba.

Fringed bleeding heart is native to the South and has more elongated, lighter pink blossoms than common bleeding heart. Its blooms are also more crowded on the flowering stem, tending to lose the attractive effect of common bleeding heart's blooms. Although most gardeners prefer the rounded flowers and more graceful habit of common bleeding heart, fringed bleeding heart does have two superior qualities: it continues to bloom sporadically on branched flower stems throughout the summer, and the foliage does not die back until autumn unless the soil dries out. This makes it an excellent summer ground cover for shady areas.

Hybrid selections of fringed bleeding heart include Luxuriant, a 15-inch-tall plant named for its lush, green, long-lasting foliage; it has deep reddish pink blooms that appear sporadically through summer. Boothman's Variety has light pink flowers. Snowdrift has white blossoms and gray-green foliage.

Planting and Care

Bleeding heart needs moist, acid soil rich in organic matter. Before planting, work plenty of sphagnum peat moss, compost, or leaf mold into the bed. Set plants so that the crown is slightly above ground level and not covered with soil. If you purchase plants through the mail and they arrive with bare roots, set them out immediately.

Partial shade is also a requirement; if not shaded, the foliage will burn. Water bleeding heart frequently during dry weather; even the long-lasting foliage of fringed bleeding heart will die if the soil dries out.

Bleeding heart will continue to bloom for many years without being divided, but if you want to start new plants or give them away, you can take root cuttings in summer or fall. You can also sow seeds of fringed bleeding heart in late summer; the seeds will sit in the bed through winter and germinate in early spring after exposure to cold.

Fringed bleeding heart has finely cut, long-lasting foliage and blooms that are borne on branched flower stems.

AT A GLANCE

❖

FRINGED BLEEDING HEART
Dicentra eximia

Features: sprays of heart-shaped blooms

Colors: pink, white

Height: 1 to 2 feet

Light: shade

Soil: moist, rich, acid

Water: high

Pests: none specific

Native: yes

Range: Zones 2 to 8

Remarks: continues blooming until fall

Bluebell

Flower buds of bluebells emerge as a lavender pink.

A native of the Eastern woodlands, Virginia bluebells bring a rare bundle of blue to the shade garden in early spring, about the time woodland phlox and violets bloom. Lifted on slender stalks above soft, green foliage, the flowers of Virginia bluebells form pastel clusters that bow their heads toward the earth. The buds emerge a lavender pink and then deepen to sky blue as the bell-shaped blossoms open. The result is a constantly changing color combination that adds charm to a perennial border or a woodland garden for several weeks in March or April. But however beautiful, bluebells are brief; in a few weeks their foliage dies back and all signs of the plant disappear until the next spring.

In the Landscape

Virginia bluebells grow from 1½ to 2 feet in height and can be used in a number of ways. Because their foliage yellows and completely vanishes by late spring or early summer, you will want to mix them with other plants or use them in a location where the yellowing foliage does not matter.

You might plant Virginia bluebells in a natural setting, such as a large sweep along a creek bank or as underplantings for azaleas, rhododendrons, or other evergreen shrubs. Many gardeners plant Virginia bluebells with other native perennials, such as columbine, to conceal the bluebells' foliage. For a striking combination, try planting yellow daffodils or early-blooming pastel tulips with bluebells. The same bed may also hold summer ferns and hostas, whose foliage will emerge in late spring to fill the void left by the bluebells. For another look, bunch a few plants together in a place where their delicate flowers can be appreciated at close range. You can also mix them with summer annuals, such as impatiens. Place a small marker wherever you plant bluebells in case you forget they are there while the plants are dormant.

Different Selections

This plant is not easy to find in garden centers because it is available for such a short time. The best time to find it is in early spring when the plants are in bloom. Chances are, you will have to order plants from a mail-order source. Most of what is offered are seedlings of

---

AT A GLANCE
❖
VIRGINIA BLUEBELLS
Mertensia virginica

Features: ruffled, bell-shaped wildflowers in spring

Colors: sky blue, white, pink

Height: 1½ to 2 feet

Light: partial to full shade

Soil: rich, moist

Water: medium

Pests: none specific

Native: yes

Range: Zones 3 to 8

Remarks: dormant in summer, fall, and winter

the species. However, breeders have developed two cultivars, Alba, a white selection, and Rubra, a pink.

Planting and Care

Virginia bluebells are native to moist woodland soils, often near streams, and do best where there is shade, rich soil, and plenty of moisture in the spring. Given these conditions, they are among the most reliable perennials for home gardens in all but the Coastal South. They can tolerate full sun because the sun is not strong while their foliage is present.

When paired with apricot-colored tulips, Virginia bluebells make a stunning show in the spring.

If you see Virginia bluebells blooming in the forest, do not dig them up to bring home. Their tubers are deep rooted and brittle, making your chances for success very slight. Start with nursery-grown transplants that you set out in spring, or plant dormant tubers in fall. Before planting, work plenty of compost, sphagnum peat moss, or rotted manure into the soil. Plant so that the tops of the large tubers are about 4 inches below ground, and space both tubers and plants about 12 inches apart.

Once established, Virginia bluebells need very little care. Make sure they get plenty of water, and each spring before the leaves emerge, apply compost as mulch or top dressing to supply nutrients and to replenish organic matter in the soil. After the flowers fade, the foliage quickly yellows; you must leave the leaves intact to nourish the underground tubers.

Blue Star

Blue star is named for its five-petaled, star-shaped blooms.

Native to the South and the Midwest, blue star includes several species of the genus *Amsonia,* known for its steel blue flowers in the spring and, in some cases, bright yellow leaves in the fall. The show begins in early spring, when stems carrying narrow, willowlike leaves sprout from a crown at the base of the plant. When fully grown, the plant stands 2 to 3 feet tall with a 3- to 4-foot spread. Clusters of steel blue, star-shaped flowers appear atop the foliage in mid- to late spring, lasting for two to four weeks.

In autumn, the foliage of blue star changes to yellow or orange-yellow. Curiously, the leaf color is usually more intense in the South than in the North. The blossoms also make fine cut flowers. Clusters of slender, milkweedlike pods appear in midsummer and may be used in flower arrangements. And the colorful foliage can be used in autumn arrangements, too.

In the Landscape

Few perennials can match blue star's versatility in the garden. It blooms equally well in sun and light shade, and it is resilient, coming back year after year without division or a lot of fuss. It is a choice plant in a border, as an informal hedge, or for naturalizing. Blue star is open enough to let you see other plants behind it. You can combine it with peonies, irises, columbines, lamb's ears, and tulips in a sunny border. Or plant it in a woodland garden next to ferns, hostas, primroses, daffodils, and spring wildflowers.

Species and Selections

Several species of blue star are good garden flowers. All grow in Zones 3 to 9 except sandhills blue star, which is not hardy in cold climates.

Willow amsonia *(Amsonia tabernaemontana)* is named for its willowlike leaves that turn yellow in fall, just like the willow tree. It grows to about 3 feet tall. Dwarf blue star *(Amsonia tabernaemontana* Montana*)* is a selection that grows only 1½ to 2 feet tall and boasts full clusters of darker blue flowers than the species. Salicifolia is a selection with long, narrow leaves and silvery-blue flowers with white throats.

Arkansas blue star *(Amsonia hubrectii)* is a lovely plant that resembles dwarf blue star but grows slightly taller. It has thin, threadlike leaves that have beautiful yellow fall color and contrast nicely with shade-loving plants, such as hardy begonia.

AT A GLANCE

❖

BLUE STAR
Amsonia species

Features: airy, star-shaped flowers atop tall, willowy foliage

Colors: blue flowers, golden fall foliage

Height: 1½ to 3 feet

Light: full sun or light shade

Soil: moist, rich, well drained

Water: medium

Pests: none specific

Native: yes

Range: Zones 3 to 9

Remarks: excellent for naturalizing or for country or cottage gardens

Sandhills blue star, or feather amsonia *(Amsonia angustifolia)*, sports narrower leaves than blue star and tolerates drier soil. It is also called downy amsonia for the hairy new leaves that give the plant a soft, silky look. Like willow amsonia, sandhills blue star has bright yellow fall color. This is the least cold hardy of all blue stars, but it does grow well in Zones 7 to 9, enduring the hot, humid climate of the Coastal South.

A native wildflower, blue star's fresh spring blooms also make long-lasting cut flowers.

Planting and Care

Plant blue star in full sun to partial shade in rich, moist soil. Plants in shade may need to be cut back to about half their height at least once after they bloom to keep them from growing too gangly. Once you have established it, you can divide blue star in fall or spring to give away or start a new plant in another spot. However, the clumps will grow and bloom dependably for many years without being divided.

To start the plants from seed, you should sow in the fall to give them exposure to cold weather. Seeds do not germinate dependably, so it is easier to start from transplants when possible.

Blue star blooms well in sun or shade. It sparkles amid ferns and Allegheny pachysandra in a woodland garden.

Boltonia

Boltonia blossoms grow in mounded clusters on tall stems.

Boltonia is a native plant that proves summer flowers do not have to end with the sultry days of August. This mounding perennial is covered with hundreds of asterlike blooms in white, pale pink, or purple that are cool and fresh in the heat of summer. The plant's narrow leaves are nearly concealed by the flowers.

In the Landscape

In the wild, boltonia is a tall, lanky plant that many people consider too weedy to add to a garden. However, the improved selections are a bit shorter, generally 3 to 4 feet tall, and more tame. Use them on slopes, in meadow plantings, or with ornamental grasses for a natural effect. Because boltonia lightens and brightens the garden, it can draw attention to a dark corner or enhance an area that is used at night. Pair white boltonia with blue or lavender asters for a refreshing combination. Wild seedlings tend to look a bit weedy and should be reserved for wildflower gardens.

Different Selections

Snowbank is by far the most widely grown selection because it maintains a fairly compact form—3 to 4 feet in height—and delights gardeners with its mass of airy white blooms. Be prepared to support the plant by tying it in loose bundles with raffia or string to help it withstand bad weather.

Pink Beauty is a pale pink selection that is shorter than the wild species but may grow to 5 feet in height and will need staking. Its foliage has a handsome bluish cast.

Planting and Care

Although boltonia enjoys good garden soil amended with organic matter, it is quite tolerant of drought. In fact, it prefers dry conditions

---

AT A GLANCE

❖

BOLTONIA
Boltonia asteroides

Features: asterlike flowers in late summer and fall

Colors: white, pale pink

Height: 3 to 7 feet

Light: full or morning sun

Soil: rich, well drained

Water: low to medium

Pests: none specific

Native: yes

Range: Zones 4 to 8

Remarks: also does well in dry soil

to wet ones, so make sure that the soil is well drained. Plant in full or morning sun. Boltonia will tolerate afternoon shade but becomes a stronger, more compact plant in full sun. Plants grown in shade may require staking. In the Lower South, boltonia needs protection from the late afternoon sun.

Cut back half of the stems in late summer when the first flush of blooms turns brown; they will bloom again in a few weeks. A clump of boltonia will multiply at the base, making propagation by division easy. Divide clumps every third or fourth fall to keep the plants vigorous. Hybrid selections, such as Snowbank, will not come true from seed. However, the native wild type can be started from seeds collected from the plants in autumn; sow right away for best results.

Snowbank, a prized white selection, wins hearts to boltonia in late summer and early fall.

Butterfly Weed

Although named for the butterflies that are so fond of its nectar-rich flowers, butterfly weed also attracts bees.

Like other flowers that thrive on hot, windswept roadsides, butterfly weed is among the most durable plants in nature. It is also one of the showiest, blooming a hot red, orange, or yellow in late spring and summer throughout the South. The flowers, which grow on bushy plants that are 1 to 3 feet tall, last up to six weeks. Gardeners have come to appreciate this plant's stamina and the butterflies it attracts; these insects like to sip nectar from the colorful blossoms, giving butterfly weed its name. Butterfly weed is also a host plant for monarch and queen butterflies; they lay their eggs on the foliage so that the hatching caterpillars can feed on the leaves.

The blooms of butterfly weed are also valued as cut flowers, which easily last a week or more.

In the Landscape

Although it grows wild along roadsides and other hot, dry areas, butterfly weed loves the moist, rich soil of a flowerbed, forming 2- to 3-foot clumps. Plant it in combination with yellow daylilies or deep blue veronicas for impact, or with perennial butterfly bush *(Buddleia species)* or annual lantana, which are other plants that attract butterflies. Butterfly weed has deep green, leathery foliage and stiff, upright stems that give it a shrublike appearance. Use it singly as an accent in a bed of low-growing, finely textured ground cover.

Flower arrangers often include butterfly weed in a bed for cutting. Cut the blooms early in the morning or at night, and set the stems in water almost up to the flowers. Snipping flowers from the plant also increases the number of blooms.

Species and Selections

Gay Butterflies is the most popular selection of butterfly weed, made up of a mix of yellow, orange, and red flowers. Plants grow 2 to 2½ feet tall.

Swamp milkweed *(Asclepias incarnata)* is a close relative of butterfly weed and is native to moist soils from Canada to Florida and westward to Utah. Unlike butterfly weed, swamp milkweed tolerates boggy, poorly drained soil; it also grows in typical garden conditions without extra water. Its flowers are a soft white and are borne atop 3- to 5-foot-tall stems that may need staking during heavy rain. It does not have a long taproot and thus is easier to transplant than butterfly weed. The flowers of swamp milkweed are also prized for cutting. Ice Ballet is a selection that grows to about 4 feet tall.

Planting and Care

Butterfly weed will grow in full sun and poor soil, including dry, sandy sites. However, it will form larger clumps in better soil. Good drainage is also a must.

Butterfly weed is among the last perennials to peek through the soil in spring, so do not give up. It also takes two to three years to reach full size; first-year plants will be small. Container-grown plants are easiest to transplant if they are young. In the garden, the plant will develop a taproot, making transplanting difficult after a year or two. Do not dig plants from the roadside, because their taproots are mired in gravel and compacted soil. Instead, collect a few seeds from the mature pods in late summer.

Because this plant is a host for butterflies, you will find caterpillars feeding on the foliage of butterfly weed. Leave them to feed if you want to enjoy the adult butterflies; they will not affect the plant.

Starting from Seed

To gather seeds, pick an entire pod when it first begins to split. Strip the silky fibers from the seeds, and you are ready to plant. For best results, sow seeds immediately after you collect them; dried seeds do not germinate well. Seedlings will quickly develop a long taproot, so it is best to plant them directly in a garden bed. If you would rather plant the seeds in a container, transplant them into the garden or their own containers as soon as the first true leaves appear. These plants should bloom in their second season.

When seedpods turn brown and split open, rows of seeds are set free. The wind catches their silken parachutes and carries them far from the mother plant.

Butterfly weed blooms in late spring and summer throughout the South.

Candytuft

Spring transforms the glossy, evergreen mounds of candytuft foliage into frothy masses of pure white blossoms.

AT A GLANCE

❖

CANDYTUFT
Iberis sempervirens

Features: evergreen, low-growing plant with spring blooms

Color: white

Height: 4 to 12 inches

Light: full sun to partial shade

Soil: well drained

Water: low

Pests: none specific

Native: no

Range: Zones 3 to 9

Remarks: excellent plant for edgings or rock gardens

Candytuft is a hardy evergreen perennial that is tolerant of cold, heat, and drought. It bears perfectly formed white spring blooms that bring to mind after-dinner mints. The blossoms, which open in early spring, last several weeks, and some selections will bloom again in the fall. Candytuft's dark green, glossy foliage provides color, texture, and cascading form year-round when it is used as a ground cover.

In the Landscape

Because of its low, spreading habit (6 to 8 inches), candytuft is best used in edgings, flower borders, or rock gardens, or as a ground cover. For dramatic contrast in both color and form, plant evergreen candytuft as a foreground for vertical, strongly colored flowers, such as deep blue iris or rich red tulips. It also makes a handsome companion for annuals and bulbs that bloom at the same time, such as pansies and tulips. Try using white candytuft to tie together a mix of varied spring colors. For a double display of color, plant candytuft as a ground cover along the edge of a bed of taller shrubs, such as red or pink azaleas.

The glossy evergreen foliage of candytuft is a nice ground cover even after the blooms have faded. You can interplant late-flowering bulbs, such as spider lily or autumn crocus, in clumps among the evergreen leaves.

Different Selections

Several named selections of evergreen candytuft are available in a variety of sizes. Reaching a height of about 7 inches are Purity, Christmas Snow (which blooms again in autumn), and Snowflake (bearing large flowers). Two smaller selections are Pygmea (4 inches tall) and Little Gem (5 inches tall). Plants generally spread at least two to three times their height.

Planting and Care

Candytuft needs a sunny spot and well-drained soil but also tolerates light shade. You should never plant it in poorly drained soil, or the plant will rot in winter. In fact, rot is the worst enemy of candytuft, as diseases and insects are seldom problems. If the soil is very heavy, improve drainage by working in a generous amount of organic matter, such as compost or manure.

Trim your plants back several inches once blooming has stopped to keep them growing vigorously and looking compact.

Fall is the time to divide candytuft, should you want to start new plantings. Since the stems naturally spread and root easily in moist soil, simply sever the stem, lift out a piece, and plant. You can start candytuft from seed, but setting out purchased transplants or divisions is easier.

Candytuft is a good companion to thrift, a type of phlox that blooms very early in spring.

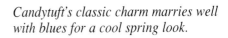

Candytuft's classic charm marries well with blues for a cool spring look.

Canna

Hybrid cannas come in a myriad of colors, including hues of the setting sun.

Tropical looking and flamboyant, canna is an easy-to-grow perennial that calls attention to the garden today just as it did years ago. From midsummer until the first frost, the flowers unfold red, orange, salmon, pink, or yellow like fluttering wings atop upright leafy stalks. The bold, upturned leaves may be emerald green, variegated, bronze, or purple, and attract plenty of attention on their own.

In the Landscape

Cannas range in height from 1½ to 8 feet, so you should be able to find the perfect one for wherever you want to make a dramatic statement. Their large leaves provide a strong, coarse texture to the landscape. In large spaces, they are perfect for massing at the end of a view across a lawn, a terrace, or other open area. Larger selections can even be used as summer screens. In smaller spaces, plant cannas in groups of three for bold texture in a flower border or next to a terrace or a sidewalk.

Avoid planting cannas in a single row; the plants appear fuller when planted in clumps of three or more. You can also mass the plants for a sweeping curve or a large, coarse textural change in a perennial border. To achieve a solid look, space the cannas 1 to 1½ feet apart, depending on their mature size.

Cannas are also bold enough to stand alone as accents in a small courtyard or a corner of a patio. They are ideal for using around water features, such as pools, ponds, or birdbaths.

A mass of cannas is most impressive when viewed across a lawn, a terrace, or another open area.

Dwarf selections remain small and will not topple, making them popular for containers. Although cannas are generally cold hardy only through Zone 7, you can grow them in containers to extend their range northward; move pots into a basement or a garage for winter.

AT A GLANCE
❖
CANNA
Canna x generalis

Features: tropical blooms; coarse foliage

Colors: red, orange, salmon, pink, yellow

Height: 1½ to 8 feet

Light: full sun

Soil: rich, well drained

Water: high

Pests: canna leaf roller

Native: no

Range: Zones 7 to 10

Remarks: tolerates soggy soil

Different Selections

Most of the cannas for sale today are the result of centuries of breeding. Old selections such as The President, a tried-and-true red, are still very popular. The Pfitzer dwarfs grow 1½ to 2 feet tall and include the brilliant Chinese Coral and Crimson Beauty. Pink President is a lovely green-leafed canna that grows about 3 feet tall. Wyoming is a striking combination of bronze leaves and red-orange blooms that tops 4 feet. Conestoga features lemon yellow flowers and is 5 to 6 feet tall. Tropical Rose is an All-America Selections winner that is easy to grow from seed (unlike most hybrid cannas). It grows 2 to 3 feet tall.

Planting and Care

Plant cannas in full sun in spring once the danger of frost has passed; set rhizomes 3 to 4 inches deep. As soon as the weather warms, the rhizomes will sprout, sending leaves up very quickly. The first blooms appear by early summer. Plants set out as late as July will have plenty of time to bloom for a late-summer and early-fall show. Although they prefer rich, moist soil, cannas will grow in either sandy or clay soil. They do not mind wet conditions and can easily grow beside a sunny stream, where they may grow taller than in a garden.

Cut off blossoms after they fade to prolong flowering. Be careful not to cut off any flowering shoots that may be coming out just below the spent blossoms. On established clumps, remove the entire flower stem, leaves and all, once its blossoms are spent; cut back to just above ground level. This thins the clump and permits light to reach any newly developing flower stems. You can also encourage more blooms by feeding with a liquid bloom-boosting plant food every few weeks from spring to fall.

Rejuvenate crowded plants by digging and separating them after the first frost in fall. Discard old rhizomes, saving the younger ones that have eyes. In areas where cannas are not cold hardy, store the rhizomes for winter in a room where the temperature stays above freezing. Pack them in peat moss or vermiculite.

Troubleshooting

Be prepared to combat the canna leaf roller, a caterpillar that rolls itself in the new leaves, chewing holes in them; these holes appear as the leaves unfold from the center of the plant. Spray at the first sign of infestation, or pick the caterpillars from the plants. See page 234 for more about this pest.

Tropical Rose is an All-America Selections winner that can be grown from seed.

Cardinal Flower

Expect vivid red blossoms and hummingbirds when you plant cardinal flower.

The blossoms of cardinal flower offer the deepest, truest reds of nature. Indeed, this plant's jewel-toned tiara will make you stop and pause if you happen upon it near a stream in the woods or a wet meadow where it grows wild.

Yet despite their bold color, the blossoms of cardinal flower are delicate, gradually opening from bottom to top with spikes on 2- to 4-foot-tall upright stalks. These progressive blooms make the show long lasting. Although the blossoms first appear in midsummer, the ones at the tip of the stalk are often still in bloom during autumn.

Cardinal flower is native throughout the South, flowering and reseeding in low areas, near standing water, and along the banks of streams. It prefers moist soil in the garden as well. While thriving in situations in which many other perennials would rot, cardinal flower can also tolerate dry soil.

In the Landscape

Cardinal flower is at its best in a landscape setting similar to its native habitat—beside a partially shaded stream or pool. It likes wet soil. A group of cardinal flowers is perfect when planted against the lush green of ferns or hostas in a woodland garden or paired with other native plants, such as a white spider lily. Cardinal flower also works well in a flower border, where it offers both strong vertical effect and enduring summer color. For some excitement in a border, try contrasting

In a setting similar to the stream banks that are their native habitat, cardinal flowers create a display that begins in midsummer and can last until fall.

AT A GLANCE

❖

CARDINAL FLOWER
Lobelia cardinalis

Features: dozens of flowers on tall spikes in midsummer and fall

Colors: red, blue

Height: 2 to 4 feet

Light: filtered sun or light shade

Soil: rich, moist

Water: medium to high

Pests: none specific

Native: yes

Range: Zones 2 to 9

Remarks: prized for long blooming time in late summer

cardinal flower with deep purple or white Louisiana iris, which also likes wet soil. Wherever you grow cardinal flower, count on visits from hummingbirds, who relish the blossoms' nectar.

Species and Selections

Native cardinal flower is often sold simply as *Lobelia cardinalis*. However, several selections are also available, including interesting red-leafed forms of Bees Flame and Queen Victoria.

Azure sage *(Lobelia siphilitica)* is a species prized for the brilliant deep blue of its blossoms. It also blooms in fall, making a spiked blue complement to goldenrod, aster, and other fall-flowering perennials.

The hybrid *Lobelia* x *vedrariensis* is an unusual purple-flowered plant that blooms from summer to fall. It has very full flower spikes that appear atop 3-foot stems and are prized for cutting.

Cardinal flowers are a striking way to add seasonal color to a border.

Planting and Care

Cardinal flowers grow best in filtered light. As with most perennials, however, the farther south the plants are, the more shade they need. If you do not have enough shade in your garden, make sure the plants get plenty of moisture, even during winter. From Zone 5 northward, cardinal flower do well in full sun.

Prepare the soil for cardinal flowers by incorporating a generous amount of sphagnum peat moss, compost, manure, or other organic material into your garden soil. Mulch around the plants to conserve moisture; be careful not to cover the foliage or it may rot during a wet winter.

The native, unhybridized cardinal flower reseeds. Transplant young plants to other garden areas, or let them grow where they appear. Cardinal flowers last only for a season or two in some gardens. For insurance, save seeds or divide plants in fall for the first few years until you see how they perform in your garden.

Catmint

Faassen's catmint begins blooming slightly later than Persian catmint.

Catmint wears a cloak of scented blue to lavender flowers from late spring through early summer. Then, when many other early-flowering perennials let you down, these heat-tolerant plants begin spreading as a handsome mound of gray-green foliage. Catmint is a relative of the feline favorite, catnip, but does not have the same intoxicating effect on cats.

In the Landscape

Related to the sages, catmints have been a traditional part of the herb garden and have long been popular in Europe. In this country, they are often planted at the front of a sunny flower border. Growing 1 to 3 feet tall, catmints make lovely edging plants. They are also a good choice for containers because they tolerate drier conditions. Plant them alone or in combination with other gray-leafed plants, such as lamb's ears, bearded iris, or snow-in-summer. Large selections brighten the back of the border, especially when combined with yellow or pink yarrow or daisies.

Species and Selections

Persian catmint (*Nepeta mussinii*) is a seedling plant that is quite lovely, with small blue or white blooms and scented leaves. Because of variability among seedlings, dividing the original plant is recommended to preserve improved selections of the species, such as Blue Wonder, Blue Dwarf, and White Wonder. Persian catmint will flower again in the fall if cut back after it blooms.

Faassen's catmint (*Nepeta* x *faassenii*) is a sterile hybrid, so it must be propagated by division or cuttings. A good ground cover or edging plant, it is long flowering but begins blooming slightly later than Persian catmint. Small, profuse lavender-blue blooms appear on upright stalks from early to midsummer and then sporadically through fall. The bloom stems are a bit stiffer than those of Persian catmint and stand up better in a hard rain. They also give the plant a more upright appearance.

You will also see named selections of catmint. Dropmore Hybrid is larger and showier than Persian or Faassen's catmint. Six Hills Giant grows to about 3 feet tall and equally wide.

Planting and Care

If it receives proper care, catmint will continue to bloom from time to time through summer and into fall. Trim off the stem tips as the flowers fade. Summer pruning helps keep the plant compact;

Catmint is an ideal choice for the front of a flowerbed. It creeps over the edge with flower-laden branches.

left unpruned, some of the lower leaves will turn brown, and the faded flower heads leave the plant looking untidy.

Choose a location that is sunny and well drained. There, plants welcome afternoon shade in the Lower and Coastal South. Although fertilizer will probably not be necessary unless your soil is extremely sandy, catmint appreciates the addition of organic matter. Organic matter, along with a slightly raised bed, also improves drainage. Good drainage is essential, especially during the winter when soggy soil can kill the plant.

The habit of catmint is to spread slowly but not too vigorously. You will probably need to divide the clump every two to three years. This is an opportunity to transplant cuttings to other areas of the garden or to share them with gardening friends.

Chrysanthemum

This blossom is typical of the fall shades for which mums are revered.

Although native to China and Japan, chrysanthemums have become an American symbol of fall that is seen everywhere from roadside stands and garden shops to grocery stores and even flea markets. Mums offer a variety of flower colors, sizes, and shapes for the garden and for cutting to bring indoors.

You may remember mums as "grandma's flowers," sprawling over flowerbeds and covered with pink, white, or yellow blooms until October, when they stand up to the first light frost. Thanks to the work of plant breeders, today's mums are more compact, bloom more heavily, and have longer-lasting flowers than their predecessors. Many bloom quite early, stretching the season from midsummer to late fall.

In the Landscape

These favorites are usually found for sale in full bloom in the fall, ready to be planted for instant color in flowerbeds and pots. You can create a sensation with only a few mums by mixing them with existing plants. Pair yellow mums with Autumn Joy sedum, purple aster, or Mexican bush sage. Mix lavender selections with gray lamb's ears, artemisia Silver King, or bright yellow goldenrod. You can also tuck in a few to enliven a bed of annuals at the end of the season.

AT A GLANCE
❖
CHRYSANTHEMUM
Dendranthema grandiflora

Features: mounds of colorful flowers

Colors: white, yellow, bronze, red, lavender, pink

Height: 1 to 3 feet

Light: full sun

Soil: light, well drained

Water: medium

Pests: aphids, whiteflies, spider mites

Native: no

Range: Zones 5 to 9

Remarks: ideal for fall flower borders and containers

At home in a large clay pot, popular Yellow Jacket mums pick up the light from taller goldenrods and make this fall border sing. At the front of the border, other mums are tucked into the bed to blend with sedum, narrow-leaf zinnia, lamb's ears, and marigolds.

A single planter with two or three mums is enough to brighten an entry.

Mums are also ideal for brightening dim areas of the garden or adding color to attract attention. Place them in front of a dark background, such as evergreens or a stone wall, to increase the visibility of the blooms.

Use them in attractive containers along a sidewalk, near garden steps, or beside an entry. If you have room for only one or two mums, put them in a decorative planter for your porch, terrace, or deck—the cheerful blossoms will last for weeks.

Different Selections

Chrysanthemums have been bred extensively; you'll find many different named selections, although the mums in garden centers are rarely named and are sold instead by color, shape, and size of bloom. You will also find very compact, small-flowered "garden mums," which are so named because they withstand rain and garden conditions better than the larger-flowered types.

Whatever mums you buy, you will find that many bloom much earlier or later in years following the season you plant them. This is because hybrid mums produced in a greenhouse are often timed to bloom at a specific time, in order to appear attractive to shoppers.

Growers in your area are generally aware of the mums that do well there; whatever your local garden center sells is likely to be well adapted to your climate. Make sure plants are not root bound when you buy them in the fall. If they are, be sure to spread out the roots before planting. (Turn to page 30 to read about dealing with rootbound transplants.) You can transplant "hospital room" mums outdoors, but they do not perform nearly as well as those that have been bred for the garden.

A mass of chrysanthemums will last about a month in the cool fall weather. You can often extend the blooming for another few weeks by pinching off the spent blossoms.

Planting and Care

You can keep many mums blooming longer by pinching the old blooms as soon as they fade. This is especially successful in the Lower and Coastal South, where fall is very long and mild.

If you have kept your mums in pots, you may plant them in the garden after they have bloomed. Following a hard freeze, cut the top growth back to the ground and cover plants with a 2- to 3-inch layer of pine straw or shredded bark. However, if you live in the Upper South or farther north, it is best to plant mums outdoors in the spring.

To keep plants free of disease, many gardeners dig their mums up every spring and plant new ones, either by taking cuttings or by separating and replanting new shoots. Mums are very easy to root. Put cuttings in potting mix, water regularly (but not too heavily), and in about a month, you will have new plants to set out. Mums need a lot of plant food; fertilize with a balanced fertilizer in March, May, and July.

While not finicky, mums require extra maintenance to retain a bushy, mounding form. Using garden shears, cut plants back by one-third in May and late July so that they will not fall over when they bloom in fall. Once flowers are nipped by heavy frost, cut plants back for the winter.

Troubleshooting

Aphids, spider mites, and whiteflies may bother mums. Turn to pages 234 and 236 for more about these pests.

Daisylike white mums bring a springtime freshness to the fall landscape.

Coneflower

Although a wildflower, orange coneflower looks nice in garden settings, too. This is the selection Goldsturm.

Whether growing wild along a road-side or sitting pretty in a flower garden, native coneflowers attract attention. Their colorful, daisylike flowers thrive without pampering from June through the first frost, putting on their best show in midsummer when other flowers are waning. Most coneflowers grow 2 to 3 feet tall and have dark green, coarse foliage; they make fine border plants with little or no coaxing. There are two main types: orange coneflowers and purple coneflowers. Both are easy to grow and make long-lasting cut flowers.

In the Landscape

Because coneflowers are wildflowers, you can mass them along the periphery of a wooded area or use them in clumps in sunny parts of a naturalistic landscape. They are particularly at home in settings where weathered wood and split-rail fences are part of the garden. They also mix beautifully in a flower border beside a terrace or near an entry. Coneflower's tall, erect form and unaffected beauty make it a graceful cut flower. And in the fall, goldfinches dine on the plentiful seed of purple coneflowers.

Species and Selections

Orange coneflowers are actually more yellow than orange. Goldsturm is the most popular selection. Its vivid color and open form make it a versatile addition to the garden. Plant it with other perennials or alone in a large mass for fresh, bright color in late summer, when other blossoms tend to look tired. A profusely flowering plant, Goldsturm is a 2- to 3-foot-tall plant with golden yellow blossoms that are 3 to 4 inches in diameter. Since this coneflower spreads by rhizomes, a planting of Goldsturm will slowly increase in size over the years; give it plenty of room.

AT A GLANCE
❖
ORANGE CONEFLOWER
Rudbeckia fulgida

Features: daisylike summer blooms

Colors: golden yellow with brown centers

Height: 1½ to 3 feet

Light: full sun to partial shade

Soil: poor to average

Water: medium

Pests: none specific

Native: yes

Range: Zones 3 to 9

Remarks: low-maintenance plants, good for beginners

The prominent cone in the center of each bloom gives this plant its name.

Purple coneflowers have perfectly spaced petals and a large central cone. The blossoms are large, as much as 4 to 5 inches in diameter. Among selections of purple coneflower is Bright Star, which grows 2 to 3 feet tall and has lavender-red blossoms with orange-bronze centers. White Lustre and White Swan are rare white coneflowers, growing about 3 feet tall and bearing white flowers that have greenish bronze centers.

There are actually three species of purple coneflower that are native to the Southeastern United States, but *Echinacea purpurea* is most often used in the garden. This perennial is hardy beyond the South, growing throughout the United States.

Planting and Care

Coneflowers are easy to grow. Although full sun produces the best growth, they will grow in partial shade, though blooming less profusely. They are well adapted to most soil types. Water needs are minimal, but keep plants well watered for best growth, especially during periods of drought. Pinching plants in late spring helps them branch out more, rather than growing tall and spindly. Fall is the best time to set out transplants.

Starting from Seed

Coneflowers can be grown from seed or divided every two to three years, preferably in the fall. If you prefer to grow your own transplants, start seed indoors in late winter. Seed can also be sown directly in the garden immediately after the last frost. In heavy or rocky soil, cover the seeds with sand to allow the tiny plants to break through the surface easily. The secret is to keep the seeds watered daily so that they do not dry out.

AT A GLANCE
❖
PURPLE CONEFLOWER
Echinacea purpurea

Features: tall, beautiful blooms; withstands the heat

Colors: lavender, pink, or white flowers with orange centers

Height: 2 to 4 feet

Light: full sun to partial shade

Soil: poor to average

Water: medium

Pests: none specific

Native: yes

Range: Zones 3 to 10

Remarks: attracts goldfinches, good cut flower

The blooms of purple coneflower rest like parasols on top of the strong, tall stems.

Coreopsis

Bigflower coreopsis is so named because its blooms are larger than those of other coreopsis species.

AT A GLANCE
❖
COREOPSIS
Coreopsis species

Features: heat tolerant, blooms from spring until fall

Colors: pale to golden yellow, pale pink

Height: 10 to 36 inches

Light: full sun

Soil: poor, well drained

Water: low

Pests: none specific

Native: yes

Range: Zones 4 to 9

Remarks: easy for beginners to grow

Gardeners who design flower borders in sedate pinks, blues, and whites often look to the excitement of yellow coreopsis for panache. These daisylike Southern natives are not only lively and pretty, but also they are tolerant of drought, are not bothered by pests, and beg only an occasional feeding. To top it off, a strategic choice among the different species of coreopsis, also called tickseed, will yield an ongoing show of bright yellow blooms in succession from April through September. For those who like the form and hardy nature of coreopsis but prefer quieter color schemes, threadleaf coreopsis offers smaller blooms, finer foliage, and pale yellow or pink flowers that add a fresh look to the garden.

In the Landscape

The eye is drawn to yellow, so take advantage of this when planting coreopsis in your garden. Use coreopsis to brighten an area, establish a focal point, or draw attention from a distance. Coreopsis blends well with reds, oranges, and other warm colors; you can pair it with a cool blue, lavender, or purple as well. Suitable blue companions include mealy-cup sage, Mexican bush sage, purple verbena, ageratum, and blue larkspur. The bright yellow or gold blooms of coreopsis bring blues to life.

Most species of coreopsis are well suited to flowerbeds that do not get much pampering, such as those that are exposed to heat near

Coreopsis breathes excitement into borders dominated by tame shades of pink, purple, and white.

a driveway or the street. They are flexible enough to grow in moist or dry conditions and work well as a ground cover in naturalistic landscapes.

Species and Selections

Dwarf-eared coreopsis *(Coreopsis auriculata* Nana) is the first coreopsis to bloom each year. It gets its name from the small lobes on its leaves that stick out like ears. Though not as widely planted as other species, dwarf-eared coreopsis has delightful flowers and a neat habit. It grows only 2 to 4 inches tall, forms a slowly spreading mat of ground cover, and will also poke its way through cracks in rocks. From early spring to the beginning of summer, it produces golden flowers that are up to 2 inches across and appear atop wiry, 8- to 10-inch stems. Dwarf-eared coreopsis, with its dark green foliage, makes a fine edging plant or addition to the front of a border.

Dwarf-eared coreopsis runs along the surface of a woodland garden in spring.

Bigflower coreopsis *(Coreopsis grandiflora)* is a short-lived perennial that grows up to 36 inches tall. Bigflower coreopsis bears 3-inch blossoms on long stems, making it perfect for cutting. It begins blooming in early summer and continues until fall. Mayfield Giant is the most popular selection, coming back each year from seed. This is a great filler plant for sunny borders or mass plantings and is a perfect addition to a wildflower garden.

In the wild, bigflower coreopsis often takes a year to begin blooming and tends to flop during rainy weather. For better performance, try Early Sunrise, an All-America Selections winner that is shorter and stockier than the species, growing only 18 inches tall. It bears semidouble blooms and lives longer; this perennial blooms from seed the first year. Another dwarf selection, Goldfink, grows about 10 inches tall and performs admirably in the front of a border. Sunray, a medium-sized plant, grows to about 24 inches tall and is more heat tolerant; it is better suited to the Coastal South. Sunray features bright yellow double blossoms on tall stems, which make striking cut flowers.

Lanceleaf coreopsis *(Coreopsis lanceolata)* looks much like bigflower coreopsis. Lanceleaf coreopsis is a little shorter, less leafy, and bears slightly fewer flowers, but its life span is longer. Like bigflower coreopsis, this plant tends to droop in the rain. Brown Eyes is a selection with single yellow flowers that have a maroon band encircling the center.

Lanceleaf coreopsis offers a bold splash of color in the garden all summer long.

Noted for its finely dissected foliage, threadleaf coreopsis is the most drought-tolerant species.

Threadleaf coreopsis *(Coreopsis verticillata)* is probably the toughest and most drought tolerant of all species of coreopsis. Named for its fernlike, finely dissected foliage, it is **stoloniferous,** spreading underground to form ever-widening clumps, and blooms the entire summer. The most popular selection, Golden Showers, forms 18- to 24-inch mounds of buttercup-yellow blossoms. Zagreb, a dwarf form, grows about 18 inches tall with deep yellow flowers. Gardeners also love Moonbeam, with its blooms of pale yellow and other soft shades.

Pink tickseed *(Coreopsis rosea)* has the same growth habit and fine foliage as threadleaf coreopsis but offers a new color palette—rosy blooms with bright yellow centers. It prefers moist soil and is well suited to sunny areas near water. Group two or three plants together for a showy clump, or plant pink tickseed in a container, such as a hanging basket, for an airy show of blooms.

Plains coreopsis *(Coreopsis tinctoria)* is an annual that should not be confused with its perennial cousins.

Planting and Care

Plant coreopsis in full sun to partial shade, depending upon the selection. It prefers poor but well-drained soil. Avoid poorly drained, heavy clay; if planting in heavy soil, raise the level of the bed to provide good drainage. Feed only once in late winter or early spring with a controlled-release flower food. Be sure to remove spent flowers during the blooming season to prolong flowering and to keep plants neat and healthy.

Save seed from bigflower coreopsis and divide other species of coreopsis in spring or fall every two years.

Dahlia

Dahlias need a little more attention than many other flowers, but the brilliant color and size of their blooms make them worth the extra care. They are sure to capture attention in a border and in flower arrangements. Although the tall types with dinner-plate sized blossoms are the best known, dahlias actually range from 1-foot-tall dwarfs with 2- and 3-inch blossoms to 6-foot types with giant blooms of 8 to 10 inches in diameter. Their colors include neon shades of red, orange, yellow, pink, as well as deep burgundy, purple, white, and bicolored blossoms. Native to Mexico and Guatemala, dahlias aren't bothered by the humid summers of the South and will bloom from summer until frost.

In the Landscape

Large dahlias are best used in a mixed border or bed where their blossoms can tower over other plants; these companions also fill in the open base of the taller dahlias. In late summer and fall, they look good with ornamental grasses, butterfly bush, perennial sunflowers (*Helianthus*), and asters. Bedding-size dahlias are compact plants that you can use in masses or in smaller clumps among perennials or smaller annuals that coordinate or contrast with the colors of the dahlias. Good choices include ageratum, gomphrena, celosia, and pentas (*Pentas lanceolata*).

Planting and Care

Plant dahlias in late spring, about two weeks after the last frost. They need at least half a day of sun to bloom well. Although the smaller selections are found as bedding plants, the grand, large-flowered types are planted from potato-like tubers that are packaged like bulbs. Set the tubers in fertile, well-drained planting holes, 3 to 6 inches deep. At first, just barely cover the tuber, but fill the hole with soil as the plants reach 4 to 6 inches tall. Tall varieties need staking because the big blossoms will make them top heavy. Drive a stake into the ground next to the tuber at planting time. Mulch over the planting to keep out weeds and keep the soil moist.

Fertilize dahlias with a low nitrogen formula such as 6-12-12. Higher nitrogen makes the stems weak. Work the fertilizer into the soil at planting and, later, beneath the mulch. Water regularly during dry weather.

Usually grown as perennials in the Lower and Middle South, dahlias need special care farther north. To protect prized selections, dig up the tubers carefully after the first frost. Use pruning shears to cut off the browned tops. Wash or gently brush soil from the tubers; let them

Dahlias bloom in summer but reach their peak when weather cools in early fall.

AT A GLANCE
❖
DAHLIA
Dahlia hybrids

Features: vivid blossoms up to 10 inches wide

Colors: red, orange, yellow, pink, burgundy, purple, white, and bicolored

Height: 1 to 6 feet

Light: full sun to partial shade

Soil: rich, well drained

Water: medium

Pests: spider mites, mildew

Native: no

Range: Zones 4 to 10

Remarks: make excellent cut flowers, tall types need staking

Dahlia

Dahlias are best known for the sheer size and bright colors of their blossoms.

dry for a few days before storing them in a cool, dry place. Put them in mesh produce bags, or pack them in a box filled with dry peat moss.

Selections

There are hundreds of named dahlia cultivars which vary in height, flower size, color, and form. Giant (dinner plate) selections that grow to more than 4 feet tall include Lilac Time, Mrs. Eileen (orange), Thomas Edison (red), and dozens of others. Others that grow equally tall, but whose flowers are closer to the size of saucers than dinner plates include Rosella (pink) and Jean Marie (two-tone purple and white). Semidwarf selections for bedding and containers, such as rose pink Ace of Hearts and yellow Suzette, grow about 20 inches tall. Most dwarf varieties, including Figaro and Rigoletto, grow only 1 foot tall, and can be sown from seed in early spring or purchased as bedding plants.

Troubleshooting

Dahlias are bothered by spider mites during dry weather, and their leaves have a tendency to mildew during damp weather. See page 236 for more about spider mites.

Daisy

Daisies are perhaps the most familiar of all flowers, cheerfully bobbing in gardens around the country. Although many flowering plants are called daisies, one genus, *Chrysanthemum*, contains many of the best-known and most dependable daisies. Botanically, a daisy is a composite flower with a well-defined center and a skirt of ray flowers that are the petals of the bloom.

These flowers have a simple appeal that marries well with stronger, brighter flowers in beds and borders. Their flat, round blooms contrast nicely with the upright vertical spikes of salvia or larkspur, and the daisies' yellow centers come to life when mixed with yellow pansies.

In the Landscape

By planting several types of daisies, you can have a succession of blooms from spring until fall. Taller daisies are effective when grouped near the middle or back of a mixed flower border, where they break up competing colors with their sunny white blooms. Because they are tough, they are good to use when naturalizing a wildflower garden, a meadow, or an area that receives little attention. They make classic mailbox plantings and work well along picket or split-rail fences. The blooms are prolific, allowing you to enjoy as many bouquets of cut flowers as you choose to cut.

Species and Selections

Shasta daisy *(Chrysanthemum x superbum)* is probably the best-known daisy. Shasta daisy blooms in late spring and early summer. It is available with single or double flowers and ranges in height from 15 to 30 inches. The foliage is deep green and is evergreen in the Lower and Coastal South. Aglaya and Diener's Double offer double flowers, while Miss Muffet is a single-flowered dwarf selection.

Daisies make excellent cut flowers.

The yellow centers of Shasta daisies are a perfect match for deep yellow pansies.

AT A GLANCE
❖

DAISY
Chrysanthemum species
and hybrids

Features: white flowers with yellow centers bloom from spring to summer

Colors: white, pink, or yellow

Height: 8 inches to 3 feet

Light: full sun

Soil: moderately fertile, well drained

Water: medium

Pests: none specific

Native: no

Range: Zones 4 to 9

Remarks: old-fashioned, cheerful perennials

Sturdy perennials, Shasta daisies highlight a sunny border.

Polaris is single-flowered with 5-inch blooms. Alaska is named for its extreme cold hardiness, growing to Zone 3; it has 3-inch flowers on 3-foot stems. Wirral Pride's flowers have short, wide petals. Shasta daisies form large clumps and live from two to three years, so divide them every other year. Shasta daisies suffer in the heat and humidity of summer; for the best performance in the Lower South, choose compact, early-blooming selections. The length of their blooming season depends upon the selection you choose, area weather, and your faithfulness in removing the faded blossoms.

Oxeye daisy (*Chrysanthemum leucanthemum*) is the earliest blooming daisy. Its white blooms continue for two to three months, from early to late spring. Oxeye daisy prefers average soil; in richer conditions, it is apt to require staking. A prolific reseeder, oxeye daisy is easy to dig and give away. Fall is the best time to dig seedlings or to divide the parent plant. An improved selection named May Queen offers sturdier stems and is less likely to reseed. The more blooms you pick, the more you get.

Feverfew (*Chrysanthemum parthenium*) is an old favorite. These aromatic yellow daisies are tiny and plentiful, and their blooms will continue all summer if you keep cutting them. Reaching 1 to 2 feet tall, they are ideal for summer arrangements. The single-flowering feverfew is a prolific reseeder; flore-pleno is a double-flowered selection. Pinch back plants if they grow out of control.

Nippon daisy (*Chrysanthemum nipponicum*) is a 2-foot-tall plant that blooms in autumn. These stems, unlike those of other daisies, are woody and bear coarse, stiff foliage. The result is foliage interest all summer and white blossoms in fall.

Clara Curtis (*Chrysanthemum* x *rubellum*) is a hybrid chrysanthemum that bears stunning pink blooms with yellow centers. It blooms in the summer and continues through fall if you remove the faded blooms. Plants grow 2 to 3 feet tall.

Planting and Care

Daisies thrive in full sun or light shade. Moderately fertile, well-drained soil is ideal. Daisies need moisture for strong growth and long-lasting flowers, especially during the hottest part of the summer. Cut back plants after they bloom to keep them tidy. Even when not in bloom, their attractive green rosettes make an attractive ground cover.

Seedlings that appear in summer may not survive the heat; those that sprout in fall can be transplanted within the garden.

Daylily

aylilies have been called the lazy gardener's flower because few perennials give so much for so little. But this depends on which daylily you choose. Of the hundreds of selections, some are grown strictly for their outstanding, prize-winning flowers, while others are perfect for durability in the landscape. If you choose your daylilies carefully, it is possible to enjoy them six to ten months of the year.

Thanks to plant breeders, daylilies are no longer limited to the tawny daylily, the well-known tall plant with orange blooms that is found along roadsides and at many old homesites. Today's hybrids come in nearly every color—cream, yellow, orange, apricot, pink, lavender, red, near-black, and bicolors. Even when daylilies are not in bloom, the fan-shaped foliage of many selections lends its green, grassy, curving lines to the landscape. And once they have put their hardy roots down in well-drained soil, the toughest selections require very little care, only occasional division.

Although the bloom lasts only a day, each *scape* (flowering stalk) has several flower buds that bloom in succession.

In the Landscape

Daylilies are classics in a cottage garden when planted in drifts in a border of mixed flowers or shrubs. Tall selections (3 to 4 feet) work best at the back of the border or against a wall or a fence. Combine them with other tall perennials, such as phlox, boltonia, New England asters, or daisies. Lower-growing selections (15 to 24 inches) add impact when planted in neat clumps and are often used in foundation plantings. Daffodils and daylilies are ideal companions; the

Few flowers rival daylilies for giving so much beauty from so little attention.

AT A GLANCE

❖

DAYLILY
Hemerocallis species and hybrids

Features: showy blooms, grassy foliage

Colors: yellow, orange, pink, mauve, red, purple

Height: 8 inches to 4 feet

Light: full sun to partial shade

Soil: well drained

Water: medium

Pests: aphids, spider mites, slugs, nematodes, thrips

Native: no

Range: Zones 3 to 10

Remarks: easy summer color, good for ground cover

Lemon-yellow daylilies light up the summer garden when planted in masses against the backdrop of perennials and shrubs.

Daylilies spread rapidly, bloom repeatedly, and make a good ground cover.

Old-fashioned favorites, daylilies make themselves at home with other wildflowers in cottage or country gardens.

daffodils bloom first, and then the daylily foliage comes up to hide the daffodil foliage as it begins to yellow.

Daylilies are also popular for mass planting, and many of the tougher selections will spread dependably to naturalize an area or to form a stable ground cover. Because their roots help stabilize the soil, daylilies are effective ground covers on steep slopes in full sun. Compact selections (8 to 16 inches) work well in containers on decks and patios or used for spots of color near stairs, doorways, or garden features. Select fragrant daylilies to plant near a favorite outdoor sitting area.

Species and Selections

The most difficult part of gardening with daylilies is choosing the right plant for your needs. Local daylily societies can usually tell you which ones grow best in your area. Daylilies are bred for different purposes; each selection is derived from different parent plants, so one daylily is better suited to a cold climate than another, for example. Generally, dormant daylilies require some cold weather, while evergreen types do better in the South. But there are exceptions to this rule—another reason to inquire locally.

Many of the beautiful blooms you see in catalogs come from selections that require more pampering and are grown strictly for the flower. Typically, such daylilies are in bloom for only three weeks, while tougher landscape selections bloom for much longer. If you are looking for exquisite large blooms in unusual colors to fit a spot in a perennial border, look to the fancier hybrids; keep in mind that they will need a bit more fertilizer and water than the tough landscape daylilies that you can plant and almost forget once they are established.

Tawny daylily *(Hemerocallis fulva)*, a dusty orange daylily naturalized throughout the South, is the one you probably remember from your grandmother's garden. It works well in a cottage garden or a wildflower setting and is very tough. Most gardeners will be happy to share theirs with you, so ask around before you buy. Tawny daylily is very tall with scapes up to 4 feet tall when in bloom. It blooms for two to three weeks in early to midsummer.

Lemon lily *(Hemerocallis lilio-asphodelus)* is also known as *Hemerocallis flava* and is another beloved, old-fashioned daylily. It features pale yellow blooms atop 3-foot scapes, has a delicate lemon fragrance, is long lasting, and spreads rapidly. Pair it with blue or white blooms, or use it in a mass planting by itself.

Reblooming daylilies *(Hemerocallis* hybrids) are a group of hybrids that are bred for their ability to rebloom through the warm months. Also included are the rugged landscape daylilies, so called for their durability, ability to multiply, and longer season of bloom. Stella de Oro has set the standard for reblooming landscape daylilies, winning points for its flushes of golden yellow flowers from late spring through fall, provided that it is not stressed by drought. However, it does not rebloom dependably in Zones 8, 9, and 10. This selection is compact, about 24 inches tall, and will grow in a container. Happy Returns, a new hybrid of Stella de Oro, is even smaller (15 to 18 inches) with a more lemon yellow flower and the same long bloom time.

Black-eyed Stella is a golden yellow reblooming daylily noted for its maroon eye, a departure from the standard landscape daylily, which is typically solid orange to yellow. Black-eyed Stella has surpassed Stella de Oro in its ability to produce many blossoms in hot climates. When given adequate water and fertilizer to supply nutrients for an extra-long growing season, it blooms for eight or nine months in Zones 9 and 10. It is also hardy enough to grow in the

It is hard to beat daylilies for bold summer colors like this pure red, which breeders have worked hard to capture.

Tawny daylily, which grows naturally throughout the South, can look quite elegant in a formal planting.

Carol Colossal is a spidery yellow daylily.

Disco Rose has a unique color combination.

same cold climates as Stella de Oro and blooms for the duration of the warm season.

Other popular reblooming hybrids include Bitsy, a dwarf yellow, Green Glitter, a tall yellow with a green throat, and Becky Lynn, prized for rose-colored blooms atop 2-foot-tall stalks. When choosing daylilies for ground cover, select those that multiply rapidly and vigorously. These rebloomers also spread rapidly: Aztec Gold, with thin golden petals; Nashville Star, with thin, red petals; and Irish Elf, with lemon yellow blooms on 1½ foot scapes. Black-eyed Stella also multiplies quickly.

Fancy daylilies (*Hemerocallis* hybrids) are the hybrids for perennial borders and for showy displays. This group includes the majority of hybrid daylilies that have been bred by daylily fanciers for color and form. Read catalog descriptions carefully and check with your local daylily society before you buy to be sure that the one you are considering is adapted to your climate.

Planting and Care

Daylilies like well-drained soil with plenty of organic matter, but they also flourish in sandy or clay soils. Good drainage is the only absolute requirement. A raised bed is one easy way to accomplish this. Full sun produces the maximum number of blooms, but daylilies also perform well in partial shade. In fact, deep red and purple selections need protection from the afternoon sun.

The daylily show in summer features a concert of color, form, and size.

Daylilies do fine with little fuss, but you will have larger, more profuse flowers if you pamper them. Each fall, improve the soil by working in good topsoil along with compost and leaf mold. Fertilize in early March and again several weeks later with cottonseed meal, alfalfa meal, or a controlled-release chemical fertilizer to improve the soil and release nutrients slowly. Then, as plants begin to bud, sprinkle ¼ cup of controlled-release flower food around the plants; this extra nitrogen produces larger flowers and more vivid colors.

To keep daylilies looking neat, remove the spent blooms from the day before. Many gardeners also clean up decaying foliage and cut scapes back once the flowers have ceased blooming in order to conserve the plants' energy.

During summer droughts when plants are blooming, give them plenty of water. Every couple of years, divide daylilies in the fall to create new beds, or share them with friends. You can dig plants and divide them at any time, provided the ground is not cold or frozen. It is best not to move them in July or August when it is quite hot. Ideal times for planting and transplanting are early to midspring and early to midfall.

Troubleshooting

Daylilies are remarkably trouble free. But when pests do strike, they can be deadly. Watch out for aphids, slugs, and spider mites. Turn to pages 234 and 236 for more about these pests. Nematodes and thrips may also be problems.

Although each flower lasts only a day, each scape features subsequent blooms in rapid succession to continue the color.

Delphinium

AT A GLANCE

AT A GLANCE

❖

DELPHINIUM
Delphinium hybrids

Features: towering flower
spikes

Colors: blue, white, pink,
lavender

Height: 3 to 6 feet

Light: full sun to partial shade

Soil: rich, well drained

Water: medium

Pests: root rot

Native: no

Range: Zones 3 to 8

Remarks: prefer neutral pH,
short-lived in the South

Stately delphiniums command attention when in full bloom.

The spires of blossoms produced by delphiniums in early summer are the dream of many gardeners. Delphiniums come in blue, lavender, pink, and white, but it is the blue that is most admired. When in full bloom, just three or four spires will capture the attention of anyone who looks their way. Because these flowers prefer cold climates, they may behave as perennials only in the Upper South. However, with proper timing, you can grow them as annuals in most all Southern regions of the United States.

In the Landscape

The classic border flower, delphiniums flower among a mix of annuals and perennials in New England gardens. In the South, poppies, foxgloves, sweet William, and other spring bloomers are good companions for delphiniums because they bloom about the same time. In the Upper South, plant flowers with dense foliage on the south side of delphiniums. This shades delphinium's roots during summer, keeping them cool and moist.

Planting and Care

Except in the Upper South, delphinium plants may be difficult to find at garden centers; some mail-order companies sell container-grown plants in the fall. You can start your own seedlings in early fall by sowing the seeds in containers kept in a cool, dark place. When the seedlings are 1 inch high, transplant them to 4-inch pots. Keep plants outdoors in light shade; water and feed them regularly. Use a liquid fertilizer, such as 20-20-20, every second or third watering.

In the fall, set out transplants in the garden in a sunny location where the soil is well drained. Delphiniums are very susceptible to root rot in soil that doesn't drain properly. Work in plenty of compost or other organic matter and controlled-release flower food at the rate recommended on the label. Delphiniums do not like acid soil, so add lime to raise the pH to about 7.0. Pinch back seedlings to encourage them to develop multiple flower spikes. When the spikes emerge in the spring, stake plants securely. After the flowers fade, pull up the plants if you are growing them as winter annuals. In the Upper South, cut off the faded blooms so that the plants do not produce seed. Mulch and water the plants regularly. In fall when the plants are killed back by frost, cut off the browned tops. Look for new foliage to appear from the crown of the plant in late winter. Where summers are not too hot and muggy, delphiniums will often return for a repeat performance the next spring.

Different Selections

Pacific Giants is a series of hybrids that grow to 6 feet tall, with huge flower clusters nearly 2 feet long. These are among the most spectacular but also the most temperamental, often lasting only two to three years even in ideal climates. Belladonna hybrids reach about 4 feet in height and hold their blooms a little longer in hot climates than do other hybrids.

Shorter selections include Pennant, Connecticut Yankees, and Magic Fountains. Usually less than 3 feet tall, these plants may not need staking. Butterfly, a blue selection, is more heat tolerant than most.

You may also see some other plants labeled *Dephinium ajacis*, but they are actually larkspur *(Consolida ambigua)*, a spring flowering annual that is related to delphinium. Larkspur is a good substitute for delphinium in the South. It is best started from seed in the fall because it has a taproot that resents transplanting.

Each blossom of delphinium is a delicate, beautiful object. Towering over other plants like a steeple, these blossoms are the fancy of many gardeners.

Dianthus

AT A GLANCE
❖
DIANTHUS
Dianthus species

Features: clouds of carnation-like flowers in spring, summer, and fall

Colors: pink, salmon, purple, red, white

Height: 3 to 24 inches

Light: full or at least a half day's sun

Soil: well drained, neutral

Water: medium

Pests: none specific

Native: no

Range: Zones 4 to 8

Remarks: handsome, fine-textured, evergreen foliage

Dianthus is a family of classic cottage-garden flowers that includes both new hybrids and old favorites. These perennials are also called pinks because they look like airy drifts of pink. If you match the right selection with the right spot, you will enjoy spring, summer, and fall blooms in candied colors that also include red, white, purple, and bicolors as well as evergreen foliage.

Dianthus are actually hardy cousins of the carnation; both are fragrant and have delicate, toothed petals. But dianthus blooms are smaller, 1 to 2 inches in diameter, and may be either single or double. Dianthus prefers a sunny, well-drained location and is undaunted by a dry summer. However, it may fall victim to stem rot in warm, rainy weather, and gardeners in coastal areas may have difficulty growing most types.

In the Landscape
Use dianthus at the front of a flower border or to spill over the edge of a pot or rock wall. A few widely spaced transplants will grow into a carpet of foliage. During winter, the hardy foliage of gray-leafed dianthus appears quite blue, contrasting against the subdued shades of the season. Low-growing selections are excellent ground covers and can be trimmed back after they bloom so that the planting remains thick. Cascading dianthus looks good in hanging baskets. Evergreen dianthus is an asset in a rock garden.

Species and Selections
If you are looking for dependable dianthus, there are several species and selections you can usually count on for your garden. The more than 200 species of *Dianthus* include annual, biennial, and perennial selections. The annual *Dianthus chinensis* is what you see every

spring in cell packs at the garden center. These are tough, pretty plants, some of which overwinter in Zones 7 and farther south, but they are not reliably perennial or evergreen. Another old-fashioned dianthus is the biennial sweet William (*Dianthus barbatus*). If planted in the fall, it will reward you with stunning blooms the following May. (See pages 128 and 129 for more information on sweet William.)

For perennial dianthus, look for some of the following selections.

Cottage pink *(Dianthus plumarius)* is both heat and drought tolerant. The foliage grows into a mat of blue-gray leaves that is just as attractive as the flowers. In late spring, cottage pinks are transformed into a cloud of sweetly fragrant little flowers. As the blossoms fade, pinch them off to keep the plant tidy.

Allwood hybrids *(Dianthus* x *allwoodii)* bloom repeatedly through the summer and are long-lived. On a sunny day you can smell their fragrance in the air.

Even when not in bloom, dianthus makes an excellent evergreen ground cover.

Cottage pinks encircle a sundial to form the focal point of this herb garden.

Dianthus

From the seeds of Allwood you will have a mixture of flower types and colors. There are many good selections including Helen (deep pink), Doris (salmon pink with a deep pink eye), and Aqua (a lovely, pure double white).

Cheddar pink *(Dianthus gratianopolitanus)* blooms in late spring and early summer with a show of color that lasts about a month and a half. Plants grow into a tight mat of gray foliage that bears fragrant flowers. The selection Bath's Pink is by far the most popular of the cheddars. Growing about 10 inches high, it has a soft pink bloom and fine-textured, blue-green leaves. Bath's Pink does not become woody or sparse in the center, rot in wet weather, or succumb to the cold. In fact, it looks good practically all year long, serving as a colorful alternative to junipers and other ground covers.

A fine choice for the foreground of a mixed border, Bath's Pink creeps over the edge of a low, stacked wall.

Only 4 inches tall, Tiny Rubies is a rich, double dianthus that covers itself with red blooms for 3 weeks in June. It is catching on with fans of dianthus and is one of the best for humid coastal regions.

Maiden pink *(Dianthus deltoides)* has green foliage and pink-to-rose flowers. This plant colors the garden for about two months, beginning in late spring. Selections include Albus (white, with single flowers) and Zing Rose (loads of rose-red blooms from late spring until frost); these grow only about 6 inches tall.

Planting and Care

Give dianthus full sun for best flowering. It demands perfectly drained soil but is not choosy about clay or sand.

There are several ways to introduce dianthus into your garden. One is to buy transplants to set out in fall. Another is to obtain divisions from other gardeners. You can also grow your own plants from seeds; either start them indoors and transplant the seedlings, or plant the seeds directly in the garden in the fall.

Prepare the soil by adding organic matter. Acid soils will also need some lime or bone meal to raise the pH to 6.5 or 7.0, so you may want to have your soil tested.

Unlike many other perennials, pinks should not be mulched; mulching holds moisture around the stems and encourages rot.

The double white flowers of this dianthus are especially soothing against the green foliage of bearded iris.

Gaura

The delicate, moth-shaped flowers and pink buds of gaura show off all summer long.

Gaura, a pretty, native perennial, is not flashy, but its faithful sprays of small, white flowers win the respect of gardeners. Although native to the prairies of Texas and Louisiana, it is perfectly adapted to gardens throughout the South, even ones in the coldest extremes of the Upper South.

Gaura's long, reddish stems bear delicate pink buds that open into moth-shaped white flowers, which come and go for five or six months from midspring until the first frost. In a flower border, the blooms hover above and between more dense clumps of flowers in a snowy mass. A stalwart resistance to heat and humidity means continuous bloom; the flowering stems lengthen to reach a height of 3 to 5 feet with the passing summer days.

In the Landscape

Gaura's delicate blooms are so charming when viewed up close that the plant is well placed near steps or a walkway. However, it is more frequently used as a filler in a flower border. Its long stems are an advantage in flower borders because they stand above the mass of summer flowers, such as daylilies, black-eyed Susans, and purple coneflowers. Its bushy form also creates sufficient mass to fill a void where spring flowers have died down.

Different Selections

Most often sold simply as gaura, few named selections or hybrids of the plant are available. However, there is a pink form.

Planting and Care

Gaura blooms best in full sun but will perform in partial shade. It also likes well-drained soil. In fact, sandy soil is best; in rich organic soil, it grows too high to remain upright. Because it is deep rooted, gaura tolerates dry summers very well. Even so, it helps to deadhead most spent blossoms to keep the plant healthy and promote bloom throughout the season; some gardeners prefer to control the ultimate height with timely pruning. The first flush of bloom lasts about a month. In July, the plant can be cut back to approximately 1½ feet. The second blooming period will be shorter and thicker than the first.

AT A GLANCE
❖
GAURA
Gaura lindheimeri

Features: mass of delicate blooms

Colors: pink buds, white flowers

Height: 1½ to 5 feet

Light: full sun to partial shade

Soil: well drained

Water: low

Pests: none specific

Native: yes

Range: Zones 5 to 9

Remarks: easy to grow, tolerant of heat and humidity

This taprooted perennial propagates by seedlings that spring up around the plant; these grow to flowering size after the first year. When you cut back gaura, leave one plant unpruned so that it will reseed. Transplant seedlings while they are young, taking care not to sever the carrotlike root. Because of the deep roots, parent plants resist transplanting.

Gaura makes a strong statement in a mixed border, where it rises above other plants and creates clouds of white blossoms from May until the first frost.

Ginger Lily

The flowers of ginger lilies resemble pure white butterflies and release one of the most fragrant scents of summer.

Ginger lily has long been handed down from generation to generation—dug, divided, and planted for its fragrant late-summer blooms. Also known as butterfly ginger, the plant has upright tropical stalks of long, slender leaves. Like silken white butterflies, the blossoms cluster atop each stem, releasing a sweet fragrance rivaled only by gardenias. This scent seems to grow stronger late in the day and lingers in the evening air. Ginger lilies also last in cut arrangements. Indoors, their fragrance has even greater impact, as does their lush green foliage.

In the Landscape

Ginger lilies are decidedly tropical, due to their large size, exquisite blooms, and heady fragrance. They grow up to 4 to 6 feet tall, so place them where their palm-like foliage will be most pleasing and their scented flowers most appreciated. They are attractive in a border or as a background planting or a screen. Because they like moisture, they may be planted on a bank near a pool of water. Or place them near a door, a walkway, or stairs to treat visitors to their display. Their large leaves and vertical stalks give them a distinct shape and texture that will attract the eye even when the plants are not in bloom. You can use a clump of ginger lilies alone or surround them with tall ferns for a fine contrast at their base.

Planting and Care

Ginger lilies enjoy moist soil that is rich in organic matter, and they thrive in full sun to partial shade. Fertilize in late winter or early spring to fuel new growth. Take extra care to water plants that grow in full sun, since the large, lush leaves lose much moisture in the sun.

AT A GLANCE

❖

GINGER LILY
Hedychium coronarium

Features: stunning blooms on large, leafy plants from June to fall

Colors: white

Height: 4 to 6 feet

Light: full sun to partial shade

Soil: rich, well drained

Water: medium to high

Pests: none specific

Native: no

Range: Zones 8 to 10

Remarks: fragrant, easy to grow

These robust plants grow from underground rhizomes. In south Florida and Texas, where frosts are few, ginger lilies remain green year-round. However, even in the mildest climate you will need to cut away ragged stems to renew the plant.

Elsewhere, ginger lilies tolerate freezing temperatures as low as 15 degrees. They die back to the ground and sprout new growth each spring. To help ensure survival, cut back the brown foliage after the first frost and apply several inches of mulch. Gardeners in the Middle and Upper South may want to dig their plants each year and store the rhizomes in the basement or garage.

The stems of ginger lilies will reach 4 to 6 feet in height. Like cannas, they do not branch, and their leafy stems grow into a clump. Propagate them by dividing the rhizomes every three to four years. This also ensures continued flowering.

The large leaves and spreading, upright stalks give ginger lilies a distinctly tropical appearance.

Goldenrod

Rough-leafed goldenrod is a native species that boasts slender flower clusters, giving the plant an airy, graceful look.

This airy, golden yellow wildflower is not the hay fever villain many people think it is. Instead, it is a sturdy native perennial that displays unusual late-summer garden color. In a garden, goldenrod grows to become fuller and often showier and more vigorous than its counterparts on the side of the road. Since it is native to some of the harshest areas in the South, goldenrods can take whatever the Southern summer dishes out and still emerge fresh and beautiful for a month or more of color. There are several species; it has been grown and hybridized for years by Europeans, who appreciate its hardiness and have developed many improved selections that are available in this country.

Goldenrod's blooms have long, sturdy stems and are very useful in flower arrangements. Cut flowers last more than a week in the vase.

In the Landscape

Goldenrod's bright color and ill-founded reputation as a roadside allergen will immediately draw the eye, so use it wherever you want to call attention. (The real allergen is ragweed, an anonymous-looking green flower that often blooms next to goldenrod on the roadside.)

Goldenrod's feathery plumes provide interesting form and texture as well as color in the garden. The many species and selections vary in size from 2 to 6 feet, offering a wide choice for placement. It is versatile enough to use among wildflowers or in a more formal, cultivated garden border.

In a garden, goldenrod is a surprisingly handsome companion to other tall perennials, such as tatarian aster, phlox, deep blue

---

AT A GLANCE

❖

GOLDENROD
Solidago species

Features: bright plumes in late summer and fall

Colors: golden yellow

Height: 2 to 6 feet

Light: full sun

Soil: poor to average

Water: low

Pests: none specific

Native: yes

Range: Zones 4 to 9

Remarks: does not cause hay fever, colorful cut flower, heat tolerant

---

veronica, ageratum, or blue salvia. These golden yellow flowers also stand out against the backdrop of deep green shrubs.

In a naturalistic landscape, goldenrod may be used simply in clumps along a fence or a long driveway to imitate natural placement in the wild. Be prepared to dig and divide many of the plants if you put them in a small space—they spread by underground stems.

Species and Selections

Many goldenrod species are native throughout the United States. The following are some of the most popular for gardens.

Goldenrod *(Solidago altissima)* spreads rapidly by underground stems, so it can become invasive in a flower border. However, it is ideal for a meadowlike setting along the edge of a country property.

Rough-leafed goldenrod *(Solidago rugosa)* has graceful starbursts of gold flowers clustered along slender stalks. At heights of up to 6 feet, this goldenrod can make quite a display. Plant it in either dry or moist soil. This species does not spread rapidly so it is a good choice for a tight spot in a border. Fireworks is a more compact selection, growing only 3 to 4 feet tall.

Seaside goldenrod *(Solidago sempervirens)* is native to coastal areas, where it grows in full sun in sand and along brackish marshes. However, it also thrives in the clay soils of more inland regions. Plant seaside goldenrod at the back of your flower border since it will grow 5 to 6 feet tall. Its vigorous, spreading roots are helpful in retarding erosion at beach homes.

Dyersweed goldenrod *(Solidago nemoralis)* is a smaller species, growing about 3 feet tall. This goldenrod is especially good for hot, dry locations. Since it blooms in late summer, it should be planted with the late-flowering seaside and rough-leafed goldenrods for an extended season of bloom and a variation in plant heights.

Scepter goldenrod *(Solidago erecta)* is one of the tallest of the goldenrods, growing up to 5 feet. It boasts large, pyramidal flower clusters. Plant it in full sun, and you will have majestic golden spires in fall.

Sweet goldenrod *(Solidago odora)* is a good choice for those who enjoy scented plants. It is not the flowers that are fragrant but the willowy leaves, which have an anise scent when crushed. Unlike other species, sweet goldenrod will grow in partial shade. It blooms in late summer and reaches a height of 2 to 4 feet.

An arching clump of seaside goldenrod fills the garden with yellow plumes that can reach 6 feet in height.

Goldenmosa, an improved selection, mixes with wild ageratum, blue salvia, and narrow-leaf zinnia.

While goldenrod typically blooms and dies down to a rosette on the ground, shrub goldenrod (*Solidago pauciflosculosa*) is a woody shrub that is 2 to 4 feet tall. It grows from the Lower South into Florida in sandy soil, bearing its flowers in July. Its evergreen leaves have a medium texture, making it an attractive addition to the garden year-round. However, when grown in rich soil, shrub goldenrod becomes leggy and loses its natural form.

Hybrid selections are crosses of native species with European species of goldenrods. They include Goldenmosa, a selection that grows 2 to 3 feet tall and blooms in August and September. Baby Gold is true to its name, reaching only 1 to 2 feet tall. Peter Pan and Cloth of Gold both bloom when 1½ feet tall. Some gardeners find that native species are more vigorous and better adapted to Southern gardens than the hybrids, so try these hybrids in limited numbers until you know how they perform in your garden.

Planting and Care

Plant goldenrod in full sun in well-drained soil. No extra watering or fertilizing is necessary.

The pyramidal flower cluster is typical of many types of goldenrod, a versatile perennial for the late-summer and fall garden.

After the flowers fade, cut the stalks back to the ground; you will have a tidy rosette of foliage. Most types of goldenrod are evergreen through the winter. The tall species can be pruned to be made more compact; in July, cut them back to half their height and they will be 1 to 2 feet shorter when they bloom.

Propagate hybrid goldenrods by dividing the plants, as they multiply with underground stems. The unhybridized types can be started from seed as well as through division. Collect seeds in late fall and germinate them in warm, humid conditions (see page 38 for more about this technique).

Heliopsis

Incomparabilis, a selection of rough heliopsis, sports semidouble flowers that are excellent for cutting.

A native wildflower, heliopsis bears sunny, drought-tolerant blooms that resemble sunflowers *(Helianthus)* but are smaller, bushier, and often more suitable for a residential garden. A favorite of both beginning and experienced gardeners, heliopsis not only performs well but also multiplies, so one or two plants will go a long way. Its abundance also makes it an excellent cut flower, perfect for gathering in jars for deck parties and picnics.

Heliopsis takes its name from the Greek word meaning "resembling the sun." Given plenty of sun and a little water, it will brighten your landscape and your flower arrangements with brilliant orange-yellow flowers from June to September. Plants range from 2 to 5 feet tall with flowers 2 to 3 inches across, in singles or doubles, depending on the selection.

In the Landscape

Because of its long-blooming season and modest demands, heliopsis should be a mainstay of the summer garden. Try the taller, lankier native version in a meadow, along a fence, or in a sunny wildflower bed. Plant newer, more compact hybrids in a perennial border. The height of heliopsis makes it suitable for the middle or rear of the bed. The vibrant blossoms combine well with salvia, phlox, Shasta daisies, purple coneflowers, pink daylilies, and ornamental grasses. Even when not in bloom, its deep green foliage is a nice contrast to silver-leafed plants, such as lamb's ears, artemisia, and dusty miller.

Species and Selections

Sunflower heliopsis *(Heliopsis helianthoides)* is a native American species that is found growing wild from New York to Georgia. Reaching 3 to 5 feet in height with a lax spreading habit, it bears single yellow flowers that are 2 to 3 inches across. Its leaves are dark green and have prominently toothed edges. Its natural, unkempt form makes it perfect for country, cottage, or native gardens.

Rough heliopsis *(Heliopsis scabra)* has leaves that are coarser and firmer than those of sunflower heliopsis. Because of its smaller, more compact shape and its larger flowers, rough heliopsis is the more popular of the two. Hybrid selections include Golden Plume, with golden double flowers, and two selections with yellow semidouble blooms, Incomparabilis and Summer Sun.

Planting and Care

Heliopsis grows well in all areas of the South except South Florida. It adapts to many soils but does best in well-drained soil that is rich in organic matter. Set out transplants in either spring or fall. Heliopsis tolerates drought, but to keep it looking its best you should water weekly during summer dry spells. If you keep cutting off the old flowers, the plant will bloom until September.

The simplest way to propagate this perennial is to divide it in early spring. Divide plants every two to three years, or when they begin to produce fewer flowers. You can also start seeds indoors in late winter and then transplant the seedlings outdoors in spring. Seed from reputable mail-order sources will nearly always produce the desired selection, while seed saved from hybrid plants in your garden may produce seedlings that revert to the wild type.

Many heliopsis hybrids mix handsomely with asters, purple coneflowers, and phlox.

Sunflower heliopsis is named for its sunflower-like blooms that open in late summer.

Hellebore

Christmas rose, a white species of hellebore, faces upward in defiance of winter's chill.

Although attractive year-round, hellebores are at their best in winter and early spring. Beginning in mid- to late winter, these graceful, shade-loving perennials unfurl flowers in pearly shades of white, rose, burgundy, or green against the backdrop of their bold evergreen foliage. Up close, you can lift a blossom and behold its fine detail. The durable flowers remain intact for three to four months, adding color and consistency to a perennial bed or border; the foliage alone serves as a dependable evergreen ground cover for shady beds throughout the year.

In the Landscape

Because of their handsome and long-lasting evergreen foliage, hellebores are grown for a ground cover as well as for their blooms. Although there are several species, all of them work well planted together. In spring, hellebores produce numerous seedlings, so a planting will naturalize to cover a hillside or edge a shady path. Plant hellebores in the shade among ferns for contrast. They also work in a mixed border or near a permanent feature, such as a statue or a fountain.

The apple green bells of bearsfoot hellebores are clustered on upright stems, making a striking statement in winter and early spring.

Other good summer companions for hellebores include caladiums and deciduous ferns. A small clump of hellebores will serve as a textural accent to such stalwarts of the winter garden as Christmas fern, autumn fern, rhododendron, and boxwood. If the leaves emerge from winter looking ragged, cut away the

White caladiums brighten a mass of evergreen Lenten rose foliage in the summer.

AT A GLANCE
❖
HELLEBORE
Helleborus species

Features: evergreen foliage, winter blooms

Colors: white, rose, burgundy

Height: 8 to 14 inches

Light: shade

Soil: fertile, moist, well drained

Water: medium

Pests: none specific

Native: no

Range: Zones 3 to 8

Remarks: ideal plant for shade gardens

---

damaged foliage when the flowers appear. The new spring growth will shoot up just in time to conceal the faded flower. Do not remove the flowers or you will not have seedlings.

Different Species

Four species of hellebores are popular in the garden. Although collectively called hellebores, the individual species have varied common names.

True to its name, Lenten rose (*Helleborus orientalis*) blooms during the Lenten season, from January through April and even into May in the Middle South. This hardy perennial is the easiest hellebore to grow in most of the South. Its nodding flowers vary in color from cream to burgundy. Some flowers sport their color in charming rosy freckles around the yellow center. You will enjoy the flowers even more if they are planted along a ledge or a winding uphill path where you can see into the blooms.

Christmas rose (*Helleborus niger*) blooms about the same time as Lenten rose, sometimes later, and is more difficult to grow. Its snowy white flowers are held erect, resembling old-fashioned, single-form roses. It grows best in the Middle and Upper South.

The leathery foliage of bearsfoot hellebore (*Helleborus foetidus*) resembles a bear's clawed foot and gives this herbaceous evergreen its common name. Native to western Europe, bearsfoot hellebore grows about 1 foot tall. In January and February, pendulous blossoms, resembling bell clappers, cluster atop the foliage. The flowers are apple green with a thin, rosy edge. The two-tone effect of the flowers and foliage is sure to attract attention in the winter garden. After the seed matures, the flower stalks turn brown and can be cut off. The offspring of bearsfoot hellebore are plentiful but not numerous enough to become a problem.

Although many people consider it deciduous, green hellebore (*Helleborus viridis*) is evergreen. By January, the leaves are ragged; gardeners may choose to cut them away or leave the old foliage to disintegrate as new leaves appear in late winter or early spring. The seedlings of green hellebore may be susceptible to drought, so they need a bit more care than those of other species.

Planting and Care

Plant hellebores in the shade of pines or in a bed on the north end of your house where shade is cast all the time. Prepare your planting

Lift the nodding blossoms of Lenten rose to enjoy their rosy, freckled faces.

Sculpturally perfect blossoms of bearsfoot hellebore make it one of winter's premier perennials.

Green hellebore grows into an even mound of bright foliage and is therefore a superb edging plant.

bed by working in plenty of compost, leaf mold, or other organic matter. Hellebores prefer a neutral to slightly alkaline soil, so raise the pH to about 7.0 by adding lime. Once established, hellebores are practically maintenance free throughout most of the South. However, they do not grow well in the tropical regions of Florida and Texas.

Propagate hellebores by digging and transplanting seedlings. It may take three to four years for the seedlings to bloom, but you can enjoy the foliage immediately. Mature plants rarely need to be divided; if you want to give a plant away, dig in fall and remember that the disturbed plant may not flower the following spring.

Lenten rose is quite effective when grown in a mass. This planting is brightened by the faces of early daffodils.

Hosta

These hostas sport blue and variegated foliage—a departure from the more common green.

Hostas are some of the most durable, long-lived, and outstanding performers for shade gardens, and there is amazing diversity within the group. Depending on the type, hostas grow from 3 to 48 inches in height, and their foliage color ranges from waxy blue to bright chartreuse. In bloom, they feature slender spires of white and lavender lilylike flowers, some of which are fragrant.

Hostas will live for decades without needing to be divided. However, they do not do well in the tropical regions of Florida and Texas.

In the Landscape

Use hostas as accents, in borders, in small mass plantings, or as a ground cover. They are also good companions for ferns, caladiums, coleus, and impatiens—other summer shade lovers. When planted so that the different sizes and colors form a leafy patchwork, they create an intriguing interplay of light and texture. Hostas with bright gold or chartreuse foliage shine like a light when contrasted with deep green shades usually found in a garden. Variegated types enliven green or blue foliage with rims and swirls of gold, cream, or white. By themselves, single large hostas make striking specimen plants.

Species and Selections

The first thing to consider when choosing a hosta is leaf color. Plants can be divided into categories based on foliage color: blue, green, yellow, and variegated.

Blue hostas actually have green leaves, but a waxy coating gives the plants a blue cast that may wear off by midsummer. Mature plants in the Upper South bear leaves as large as a serving platter.

AT A GLANCE

❖

HOSTA
Hosta species

Features: long-lived plants with lush foliage from summer to fall

Colors: green, blue-green, yellow, and variegated

Height: 3 to 48 inches

Light: light shade

Soil: rich, well drained

Water: medium to high

Pests: slugs, snails

Native: no

Range: Zones 3 to 8

Remarks: mixes well with ferns for shade

Blue hostas attract attention when grown in a large clump.

Royal Standard is grown for its showy, fragrant white flowers as well as for its green foliage.

Variegated hostas brighten shady walks.

A clump of *Hosta sieboldiana* Elegans or Ryan's Big One may grow to 3½ feet tall and 4 to 6 feet wide. These plants do not get this large in the Lower South because the weather is too hot. However, they will reach 2 feet in height with an equal or greater spread. These are slow growers; it takes them 5 years or more to reach full size. Other good blues are Blue Wedgwood, Blue Skies, and Halcyon.

Green hostas may not be as interesting as those with gold, blue, or variegated leaves, but you should not discount them. Green selections still serve as excellent background plantings and ground covers, where some of the more colorful types would be too vivid. In addition, the hostas with the most fragrant blossoms have green leaves; Royal Standard, Honey Bells, and *Hosta plantaginea* have large, white, fragrant blossoms.

Variegated hostas include some of the old-fashioned hostas you see planted in established neighborhoods. A popular choice is *Hosta undulata* Albomarginata, a green plant with white margins. It is inexpensive and rugged. Among the newer choices is Golden Tiara, with green leaves and gold borders. It forms a compact mound of heart-shaped foliage and sends up lavender blossoms in early summer. Kabitan, a dwarf with straplike leaves, stays less than 8 inches tall, making it a good choice for an edging. If you are looking for a very small hosta, try *Hosta gracillima* Variegated. Instead of forming clumps, it spreads by **stolons,** or creeping stems, and is no more than

Albomarginata is one of the most popular hostas for ground cover. It is inexpensive and spreads rapidly.

3 inches tall. Frances Williams is one of the country's most popular hostas, growing 2 to 3 feet tall with large, blue leaves that have a gold outline. This selection does not like the sun; direct sun often burns its gold borders, especially when the tender new leaves appear before the shading trees sprout leaves in spring.

Yellow hostas draw the most attention with unusual gold-to-chartreuse shades, but they are not always easy to use. However, in the right place, they provide brilliance unmatched by other plants. Use the yellow hue to its best advantage by placing it in contrast with deeply colored backgrounds. One of the grandest, Sum and Substance, bears 1- to 2-foot leaves on 3- to 4-foot plants. Other good yellows are Golden Prayers, with heart-shaped, puckered leaves, and August Moon; their mature leaves are large like Sum and Substance, but their surface has a quilted texture.

Planting and Care

Hostas do well in the shade but like a little bit of sun. The best sites receive morning sun or light dappled by trees. Plant hostas in a well-drained spot with good soil to which organic matter has been added.

Hostas need plenty of water. Their large leaves absorb moisture, so keep plants well watered during dry weather.

Before you buy, check with a local garden center or a hosta enthusiast about any peculiarities regarding care. Many hostas cost as much as a small tree or shrub, so get advice before purchasing.

Troubleshooting

Be prepared to fight slugs and snails. See page 236 for more about these pests.

Yellow-leafed August Moon hostas punctuate a walkway lined with carpet bugleweed.

Iris

AT A GLANCE

BEARDED IRIS
Iris species

Features: large, ornate blooms on tall, spiky green foliage

Colors: blue, purple, white, yellow, brown, pink

Height: 8 to 36 inches

Light: full sun

Soil: rich, well drained

Water: low

Pests: iris borer

Native: no

Range: Zones 3 to 10

Remarks: easy to grow, drought tolerant, old-fashioned

The upright flowers and foliage of bearded iris contrast nicely with the rounded shapes of boxwood and the prostrate form of dianthus.

Of all the perennials, iris may be the most universally grown. In this large and varied group you will find types for hot, dry sites, shady bogs, dry shaded areas under trees, cutting gardens, or just for flowering accents. Iris come in several shapes and sizes and, if chosen carefully, can offer blooms in three seasons. Many are maintenance free, though some require pampering. All produce classic flowers and handsome foliage that may be as striking as the blooms themselves.

Bearded Iris

In mid- to late spring, bearded iris produce huge blooms whose lower petals sport a goatee of fuzzy hairs. Although the flowers come in just about every color, bearded iris are prized as much for their foliage as for their blooms. Long after the flowers fade, 8- to 24-inch-tall vertical leaves offer an attractive complement to horizontal, creeping plants, such as creeping thyme and dianthus or the more rounded form of peonies.

In the Landscape

Bearded iris are often planted in single-file borders or in beds by themselves. When these gorgeous flowers are not in bloom, you are left with formal plantings of green, spiky foliage. To avoid this starkness, incorporate iris into beds and borders with other sun-loving flowers, such as blue phlox, pansies, peonies, candytuft, artemisia, or yarrow. Some iris rebloom again in the fall; yellow and wine-colored rebloomers make good companions for fall-blooming perennials and foliage plants.

Different Selections

Newer selections of bearded iris have been bred for larger, more abundant flowers in many exotic colors. They are wonderful when cut, winning ribbons at flower shows, but they also demand more attention than some of the tougher types. For landscaping, plant tried-and-true iris, such as Arctic Fury (white), Beverly Sills (coral pink), Blue Sapphire, Carolina Gold, Debbie Rairdon (white and creamy yellow), Mary Frances (light orchid-blue), Stepping Out (purple and white), and Vanity (pink).

Iris breeders have developed a reblooming iris that blooms again in fall. These perennials come in all of the colors of regular iris and in tall, intermediate, and dwarf sizes. A few selections are Pink Attraction, I Do (white), Buckwheat (yellow), Violet Returns, and Plum Wine. But to get a fall show as spectacular as the one in spring, you must keep the plants growing vigorously throughout summer and prevent them from going dormant. Water regularly and give them plenty of food. Sprinkle a tablespoon of controlled-release fertilizer around the base of each plant in spring, just after the last blossoms fade, and repeat in midsummer.

Planting and Care

Bearded iris demand full sun and good drainage. Growing from fleshy rhizomes, these iris are surprisingly drought tolerant, requiring water only when planted and in the spring. They prefer dry soil in summer and a cool winter, thus they do not thrive in the Coastal South.

Plant bearded iris in late winter, summer, or fall. Work compost, shredded leaves, or other organic matter into the soil. Plant rhizomes a foot apart, taking care not to bury them completely. Do not cover the rhizomes with mulch; instead mulch between the iris, leaving the tops of the rhizomes to bake in the sun. Divide iris in the fall when the rhizomes become hunched and crowded. Lift the rhizomes from the ground with a turning fork, cutting away the oldest and leaving the younger ones. Each remaining section should have feeder roots and a fan of leaves.

A fuzzy "beard" on each lower petal gives bearded iris its name.

Troubleshooting

If you find leaves turning yellow, dripping sap, and dying, the culprit may be an iris borer, a caterpillar that burrows through the rhizomes. Leaves of infected plants look ragged near the base where the caterpillar first begins chewing. Discourage the pest in late summer and fall by cleaning up any old, brown foliage where a moth may lay eggs to overwinter. In spring, you can spray the lower half of the plants with an approved insecticide to kill the emerging larvae.

The spikes of Japanese roof iris stand 10 to 12 inches tall.

Japanese Roof Iris

Japanese roof iris gets its name from Japanese lore that growing it at the edges of a thatched roof brings good luck. In early spring, the plants send up 10- to 12-inch-tall spikes of lilac-blue or white blossoms with petals that are spread apart like an open-faced sandwich. When not in bloom, the arching fans of light green evergreen leaves make an elegant ground cover.

In the Landscape

Perfect for naturalizing in sun or partial shade, Japanese roof iris multiply freely to form a large mass in a few years. They are good companions for naturalizing with daffodils in a shady woodland garden. You can also use them in clumps in a sunny bed. Combine them with hellebores, daffodils, and daylilies. Unlike the more rigid leaves of bearded iris, Japanese roof iris foliage is a bit floppy, giving a softening effect to a bed or a ground cover.

Planting and Care

Japanese roof iris bloom best in full sun, although they tolerate some shade. They also need moist but well-drained soil. You can increase the size of your planting quickly by letting spent flowers form seedpods; in midsummer when the pods turn brown, open the pods, gather the seed, and sow them directly into the garden, about ¼ inch deep. Seedlings will emerge in thick stands within two months. When the seedlings reach 2 to 3 inches tall, separate and transplant them to empty spots in the garden, spacing them about a foot apart.

Japanese roof iris propagate easily enough by division, but you will get better plants and more of them by gathering and sowing seed.

AT A GLANCE

❖

JAPANESE ROOF IRIS
Iris tectorum

Features: blooms, evergreen foliage

Colors: lilac-blue, white

Height: 10 to 12 inches

Light: full sun to partial shade

Soil: rich, well drained

Water: low

Pests: none specific

Native: no

Range: Zones 4 to 10

Remarks: a great plant for naturalizing or growing in masses

Planted above a stacked stone wall, this mass of Japanese roof iris offers pristine white blooms atop elegant green foliage.

Louisiana iris punctuate the landscape with their sharp vertical form.

Louisiana Iris

Native to Louisiana's wild wetlands, this iris enjoys moist soil conditions and is popular for low, wet areas and the edges of ponds. However, they will grow almost anywhere, from soggy muck to an ordinary flowerbed. Each stalk flowers first at the top, next at the bottom, followed by two to three buds in the middle. Many bloom in early spring, but late-blooming hybrids open in mid- to late spring with the first daylilies. Louisiana iris make superb cut flowers.

The leaves, which are narrow and upright, grow 3 to 4 feet tall; in the North they are killed to the ground by a hard freeze. In warmer areas of the South, however, the leaves are evergreen and actually grow fastest in winter.

In the Landscape

Louisiana iris are popular placed in pots submerged in a water feature, planted in flowerbeds to add color and vertical foliage, or placed along the edge of a stream or pond. Wherever they grow, Louisiana iris are instantly recognized by their unique foliage and thin flower stems that may flop over after a heavy rain.

Species and Selections

Because many hybrids have been bred over the years from such parent plants as leafy blue flag *(Iris brevicaulis),* many selections of Louisiana iris are cold hardy enough for Zone 4. They represent a spectacular color range—perhaps the widest of any group of iris—including violet, blue, purple, pink, white, magenta, red, and orange. The best way to get a selection suited to your area is to check locally. Be aware that many of the selections may not be sold by any name other than Louisiana iris.

Flag iris *(Iris pseudacorus)* is a dependable, tall, narrow-leafed species grown mostly around water, either submerged in a pot or at the edge of a pond or stream. However, it also grows well in garden beds provided it is watered during periods of drought. The plant reaches 2 to 3 feet tall and bears yellow blooms in early summer. It is hardy from Zones 5 to 9.

Siberian iris *(Iris siberica)* is another excellent choice for wet sites. This iris is so versatile that it thrives in a container, in water, or in the narrow strip between a street and sidewalk. Native to

AT A GLANCE

❖

LOUISIANA IRIS
Iris Louisiana hybrids

Features: exotic flowers with green, reedlike foliage

Colors: magenta, blue, white, red, pink, orange, violet, purple

Height: 3 to 4 feet

Light: full sun

Soil: rich, moist, acid

Water: medium to high

Pests: none specific

Native: yes

Range: Zones 3 to 10

Remarks: great for ponds and water features

Known for their vast color range, Louisiana iris are among the most hybridized of the iris family.

moist meadows, Siberian iris can be planted nearly anywhere, in full sun or partial shade. The foliage is narrow and varies from 1 to 3 feet in height, depending on the amount of water the plant receives. Selections bear flowers in deep purple, various shades of blue, and white. Siberian iris grows in Zones 3 to 9.

Planting and Care

Louisiana iris need at least six hours of sun a day. (In hot, dry climates, give them afternoon shade.) Before planting, loosen the soil to a depth of at least a foot and work in plenty of organic matter. These plants prefer acid soil.

The best time to plant is in late summer or early fall when plants are dormant. Promptly unwrap the roots of plants that arrive in the mail and store them in water until you are ready to plant. Set these rhizomes at or slightly below the soil surface, spacing them at least a foot apart. If you plant in spring, keep them well watered. For a waterside planting, do not plant the rhizomes directly in the water. Instead, place them at the water's edge. Iris planted on land need no more moisture than other perennials, but if they have extra water in spring and fall, they will have better blooms.

Dwarf Crested Iris

These dainty native iris *(Iris cristata)* grow only 4 to 6 inches tall to carpet the ground in a mass of blue and yellow early-spring blossoms. One of the most dependable wildflowers for shade, dwarf crested iris will spread to form large masses when left alone. The blooms are only an inch wide. The foliage is flat and straplike, appearing in early spring before the blossoms; in fall it disappears.

In the Landscape

Dwarf crested iris grows best in a wooded setting where it can naturalize. If possible, plant these iris so you can enjoy them from a terrace or a window. Or let them spread along a shady walkway or driveway. When grown in a bed, they must be planted in masses away from heavy shade and competing roots of taller plants. Suitable companions include such perennials as wild columbine and wild ginger. Maidenhair fern also works well with dwarf crested iris, provided the soil does not get too dry for the fern.

Different Selections

Most dwarf crested iris are sold under that name. However, you may find a white variety, Alba, which is not quite as vigorous as the blue.

Planting and Care

Once established, dwarf crested iris takes care of itself, often tolerating the dry conditions under large shade trees. However, the plants bloom best if they receive some sunlight and are well watered during dry periods.

Plant in late winter or early spring in well-drained soil. Set rhizomes ½ to 1 inch deep. Each rhizome will produce three to four new roots every year. Once settled in the home garden, dwarf crested iris spreads quickly by long, thin rhizomes that creep just below the soil surface or at ground level.

You can start new plantings or dig plants to give away by separating established clumps. Dig in fall or late winter.

Louisiana iris are well adapted to boggy conditions.

Lamb's Ears

Even in the summer, lamb's ears look cool and refreshing, as if lightly frosted.

One look at the floppy, soft, woolly leaves will tell you how lamb's ears got its name. However, the appeal of lamb's ears goes far beyond softness. The silvery gray foliage is as elegant as it is interesting. The plant's mound of leaves grows 6 to 12 inches tall and stands in contrast to the green foliage or flower colors of adjacent plantings. And the 4- to 6-inch-long leaves provide a coarse, textural break as well.

In the Landscape

Although it is attractive when used alone, the greatest asset of lamb's ears is its capacity to bring out the colors of surrounding flowers and foliage. Finer leafed companion plants include the perennial dianthus and catmint, or the annual Madagascar periwinkle and narrow-leaf zinnia. It is also handsome at the base of old-fashioned pink roses, such as the Fairy rose.

While the leaves of lamb's ears are attractive all season long, the early summer flower stalks cause the plant to stretch, destroying its ground-cover effect. The leafy mat sprouts 12- to 18-inch spikes of purplish pink flowers. Pinch off the flower stalks as they begin to shoot upward, or plant the selection Silver Carpet, which never blooms. Use the bloom stalks in flower arrangements.

Different Selections

Usually sold simply as lamb's ears, this plant is not often found in a wide variety of selections at garden centers. However, if you are lucky, you may find a few that are particularly outstanding. Silver Carpet is nice because it does not produce the tall bloom spikes. Helen von Stein is prized for its large leaves and tolerance of hot, humid conditions.

Planting and Care

Put lamb's ears near the front of a bed where they will not be hidden by taller plants. Best planted in spring, they grow together during their first season. Although they tolerate partial shade, the more sun they receive, the stronger they will be. They do need excellent drainage.

To keep a clump of lamb's ears looking fresh, prune plants in late winter. The only regular maintenance required is trimming back the edges of the plants, to help keep the center of the plant full, and removing decayed leaves, which are unsightly and may encourage rot.

The purplish pink spikes bloom in early summer.

Also remove flower stalks as they appear or as the flowers fade, depending on your preference.

Lamb's ears spread so fast that you will probably need to divide them in spring or fall every two to three years. As a plant ages, new growth comes out from the tips of the stems while the foliage dies out in the center. Divide the plants by digging them up and separating the healthy stems. Even if these do not have many roots, place the stems on their sides and cover lightly with soil. Keep them moist, but not too wet.

Lamb's ears are cold hardy in the South, but gardeners in Florida and along the Gulf Coast may have problems in summer as constant heat and humidity can damage the plants, even in well-drained, sandy soil. When watering, try to keep moisture off the leaves because they tend to trap humidity, thereby promoting leaf rot. Avoid using a sprinkler, and water plants in the morning so that they have time to dry out before nightfall.

Best planted near the front of a border, lamb's ears spread into a leafy mat that grows taller just before the plant blooms.

Moss Verbena

Blooming all summer and fall, moss verbena stops flowering only at frost.

Fans of roadside flowers may recognize moss verbena as the low-growing wildflower that produces a carpet of purple flowers all summer. Even in hot, dry, windswept conditions, it just keeps on blooming, which is why many gardeners use it as a mainstay of summer beds, border edgings, and rock gardens. Unlike annual verbena, moss verbena is resistant to diseases and insects, and it is also a better garden performer.

A South American native, moss verbena is naturalized in the Lower and Coastal South, where it grows as a perennial. It can be grown as an annual by gardeners in cool areas, and it is worth replanting every spring. Similar in color and habit to moss pink *(Phlox subulata)*, moss verbena has dark, glossy foliage that grows unblemished in a lacy, green mat in full sun. Although some of this foliage remains green through winter, severe freezes will kill most of the top growth. However, new leaves sprout with the warming weather, and the plant is in bloom by May in the Middle South. Spring is just the beginning for moss verbena, whose display lasts until frost, especially if you trim back the old, spent blooms several times during the season.

In the Landscape

Moss verbena's lavender-purple blooms make an excellent combination with pale yellow flowers, such as Moonbeam coreopsis. Some gardeners prefer the white-flowered moss verbena selection called Alba, or a mix of the two.

An ideal plant for the front of a sunny flower border, moss verbena can be planted with spring bulbs. Coming into bloom about the time the bulb foliage fades, it will carry the show for the rest of the season. Use moss verbena as a ground cover on gentle slopes, in rocky soil, and in areas prone to drought. It is also a good choice for the edge of a driveway or even among the pebbles of a gravel parking court or walkway.

Because it may reseed or spread by rooting stems, moss verbena becomes naturalized in sunny gardens much as it does along roadsides. Take advantage of this, especially on large properties.

Different Selections

Few named selections or hybrids of the plant are available; this plant is most often sold simply as moss verbena.

Planting and Care

Choose a sunny, well-drained location, and moss verbena will thrive. Although it becomes leggy and thin without enough light, the only sure way to kill it is to plant it in soggy soil. When moss verbena starts looking bedraggled in midsummer, trim it back to 3 to 4 inches and it will rebound crisp and pretty. In areas where it is not perennial, you may see it reappear from seed the next spring.

Moss verbena spreads by layering; that is, the stems root as they creep across the soil. A planting of perennial moss verbena will undoubtedly get larger.

Moss verbena is the perfect summer edging plant for a walkway, lining it with a mat of color.

Peony

Peonies are quite handsome, especially in flower arrangements.

For spontaneity, exuberance, and beauty, few perennials surpass peonies. Each spring, this hardy perennial comes up from just a few roots to become a sturdy, shrublike plant covered with dense, leathery foliage and dozens of exquisite flowers. Once planted, a peony often lives for decades. Peonies are delightful cut flowers in spring arrangements.

In the Landscape

Because of their large blossoms, peonies are at their best when grown in large groups to create a mass of color. They are also effective in a perennial border, especially when contrasted with such strongly vertical plants as bearded iris and poppies.

After they bloom, these fine, dense plants serve as a background for later perennials that grow no taller than 2 to 3 feet, such as coreopsis and asters.

Species and Selections

Peonies must have some cold weather, but many selections perform beautifully as far south as Zone 7 and the northern half of Zone 8. The key is choosing a selection that blooms early. (See chart on opposite page.)

The single-flowered Japanese peonies bloom reliably. Semi-double or double forms are more likely to become waterlogged and attract disease. But if you want a double-flowered peony, choose an early-flowering one, such as Festiva Maxima, a beautiful white that does well even in Zone 8.

Tree peony *(Peonia suffruticosa)* has a woody stem that does not die back to the ground each year. It grows well in Zones 6 and 7 but needs protection from cold in Zone 5. Tree peonies also prefer neutral to slightly alkaline soil, so adjust the pH to 7.0. In the South, they require shade in the afternoon.

Most tree peonies grow 3 to 5 feet tall but may need pruning down to a foot high every few years to encourage new growth.

AT A GLANCE

❖

PEONY
Paeonia lactiflora

Features: large, full blooms top shrublike plants in late spring

Colors: white, pink, red, and flecked

Height: 2 to 3 feet

Light: full sun

Soil: well drained

Water: high

Pests: thrips, beetles

Native: no

Range: Zones 2 to 7

Remarks: live for decades

The early-blooming peonies are likely to bloom at the same time as bearded iris.

Planting and Care

The best time to plant peonies is in fall, although you can also plant them in spring. While directions will tell you to plant several inches deep, in the South the red eyes (sprouts) on the root should be placed no more than ½ to 1 inch below ground level for best flowering. Peonies resent transplanting, so plant them in a spot where they will stay.

Peonies need full sun or light shade, well-drained soil, and lots of water, especially in spring. Use only low-nitrogen fertilizer in spring; overdoing it can produce too much foliage and fewer flowers. Also, stake the plants or let them grow through a wire support early in the season to bear the weight of the foliage and flowers.

SOME EARLY-BLOOMING PEONIES

Selections	Flower Color	Flower Type
Charles White	White	Double
Dancing Nymph	White	Single
Edulis Superba	Pink	Double
Festiva Maxima	White/red flecks	Double
Krinkled White	White	Single
Lady Alexandra Duff	Pale pink	Semidouble
Largo	Pink	Single
Sarah Bernhardt	Pink	Double
Scarlett O'Hara	Red	Single

Be patient—blooms will be disappointing the first year but improve in succeeding seasons.

Do not remove more than two or three leaves with a stem; the plant needs its foliage for steady growth. If you need long stems with more foliage, cut no more than half of the flowers on the plant. If you want extra-large flowers for arranging, pinch off the buds that develop along the sides of the stem as soon as they appear, allowing only the terminal bud to develop.

Troubleshooting

Thrips (thin, black insects smaller than a grain of rice) and beetles can ruin the blooms. Cut back the foliage each fall after the first hard freeze to prevent the spread of disease.

Tree peony is a woody plant that does not die back to the ground in winter the way other peonies do.

Single-flowered peonies are less likely to be damaged in a rainstorm than the double-flowered types.

Phlox

A delight in early spring, woodland phlox dots roadsides, meadows, and mountainsides. This native is easy to grow, offering striking lavender-blue flowers that spruce up perennial borders and bring early spring life to shady beds and wildflower gardens.

Woodland phlox thrives throughout the South, except in the southernmost areas of Florida and Texas. The blossoms are slightly fragrant and appear from early to midspring in time to mix with daffodils and other early blossoms. The blooms are about 1 inch wide and are borne in clusters atop foot-long stems. Colors range from lavender-blue to pale violet and white. The display lasts about three weeks, and then the flowers form seeds, which self-sow to thicken the planting. Leaves often turn brown shortly after the blossoms fade; new leaves appear in late summer or early fall.

In the Landscape

Woodland phlox has a low, mat-forming habit, making it an excellent woodland ground cover. Combine the plant with others in rock gardens and flower borders, but do not put it in prominent spots by itself. The plant is not very attractive in late spring when the flowers go to seed or in midsummer when the foliage is brown. Consider interplanting woodland phlox with spring bulbs, such as daffodils or tulips, or mix it with hardy ferns to camouflage it during these times.

The blue shades of woodland phlox are strong enough to hold their own among bolder colors. This plant combines well with bright hyacinths, bearded iris, and yellow pansies or primroses.

In a more formal, cultivated border, woodland phlox makes a good companion to bulbs.

AT A GLANCE

WOODLAND PHLOX
Phlox divaricata

Features: early spring blooms

Colors: blue, violet, white

Height: 8 to 15 inches

Light: partial shade

Soil: moist, rich

Water: medium

Pests: powdery mildew if stressed by drought

Native: yes

Range: Zones 5 to 9

Remarks: reseeds, requires little care

Woodland phlox is perfect for lining a shady walk.

Species and Selections

Woodland phlox comes in many shades, from true blue to nearly pink. It also comes in white. Many of the wild forms have the slightest hint of pink, although there are actually no true pink selections. Plants that are raised from the seed of native species may vary in color. Named selections are propagated from cuttings and should be consistent in color. Dirgo Ice is a pale lavender-blue form about 8 to 12 inches tall. Fuller's White is more tolerant of sun than most other selections; it also blooms a bit longer, often lasting over a month. Louisiana Blue is an early-flowering purplish blue phlox.

For larger flowers, try Laphamii (*Phlox divaricata* Laphamii), a subspecies with blue-violet flowers that lacks the characteristic notch on each petal. Laphamii tolerates more sun than other selections. Chattahoochee is a hybrid of Laphamii and another native, Downy phlox *(Phlox pilosa)*. It has a magenta eye in the center of each blue flower, and it stays in bloom longer than wild species of woodland phlox—often over a month. Chattahoochee tolerates full sun and sandy soil. It grows in Zones 5 to 9 and is not as hardy as woodland phlox.

Downy phlox blooms later than woodland phlox, mixing well with early roses or the light green of newly emerged ferns. Ozarkana is a pink selection that tolerates sun as well as partial shade. It grows in the range of woodland phlox.

Creeping phlox *(Phlox stolonifera)* is not as showy or vigorous as woodland phlox. However, it tolerates even deeper shade, making it a good choice for heavily wooded lots. This native grows from Zones 2 to 8 and is quite hardy.

Planting and Care

The best time to plant is in fall so that plants can become established before they bloom in early spring. However, you can also plant in spring when they are likely to appear in full bloom in garden centers.

Growing wild from Canada to north Florida and west to Texas, woodland phlox also adapts easily to garden conditions. It prefers dappled sunlight in spring and shade in summer, conditions found under deciduous trees. If the soil is not fairly rich, amend it before planting with generous amounts of organic matter, such as compost, manure, or sphagnum peat moss. Roots are shallow, so mulch with more organic matter to help conserve moisture.

Fuller's White offers color variation in the garden.

Woodland phlox usually survives summer drought—the plants are dormant at that time—but avoid open sites as the summer sun is too harsh and bakes the soil. Occasionally you may see powdery mildew on the leaves, especially on plants that have been stressed during a dry winter, but the plants recover on their own.

Starting from Seed

If left alone, woodland phlox will reseed and multiply. Each plant will also spread gradually to form a clump, so you can increase plantings by dividing clumps every third year in fall or spring. In fact, this is the best way to propagate hybrids, which do not come true from seed. Divide older plantings to renew them in spring just after they bloom or in the fall.

Another easy way to propagate woodland phlox is by ground layering. Bend a piece of stem to the ground, place a handful of soil on top, and weight the stem down with a stone or a brick. Rooting will be complete in about two weeks; then transfer the rooted layers to their new locations. (See page 46 for more about layering.)

As its name implies, woodland phlox is at home in a wooded setting where it can reseed and spread as a ground cover.

Primrose

In spring, the Japanese primrose blooms along tall flower stalks.

With plant heights that rise and fall like musical notes, Japanese primrose combines the colorful impact of phlox with the architectural beauty of hosta. It is also one of the easiest primroses to grow, provided it has a steady supply of water.

This plant is a boon to gardeners because of its spring blooms in shady, boggy sites, often the death of many well-known perennials. From a tuft of bright green, spinachlike leaves, it produces whorled tiers of blooms up to 2 feet tall in vivid colors ranging from white to pink to red to purple. When not in bloom, the foliage remains a handsome rosette of 6- to 12-inch-long leaves.

In the Landscape

The banks of a stream or a pond are good sites for Japanese primrose, which needs consistent moisture. It is also an excellent choice for use around birdbaths and other water features. Mass groups of a single color in the moist shade along the banks of a wooded stream, or blend purples, whites, and pinks for a more dazzling look. Also try Japanese primrose with other moisture and shade-loving plants, such as hostas, Virginia bluebells, or ferns.

Different Selections

Several garden catalogs offer mixtures of pink, rose, purple, and white, selections that return from seed in a variety of hues. For solid colors, try Miller's Crimson or Postford White (white with a yellow eye). Miller's Crimson will come back a true color from seed. Cowslip primrose, *Primula veris*, is a related plant with smaller yellow flowers. Cowslip is better adapted to garden conditions in shady beds and grows well throughout the Middle South.

Planting and Care

The soil should be acid and evenly moist, but not soggy, and should contain plenty of organic matter. If the soil is too wet, the plant may

---

AT A GLANCE
❖
JAPANESE PRIMROSE
Primula japonica

Features: spectacular spring blooms on candelabra-like stems

Colors: white, pink, red, purple

Height: 1 to 2 feet, in bloom

Light: light shade

Soil: moist, acid, rich

Water: high

Pests: none specific

Native: no

Range: Zones 5 to 8

Remarks: likes boggy conditions; easy to grow

be heaved out of the ground in winter, particularly in the Upper South. If it is too dry, it may die shortly after blooming and setting seed. If the soil is consistently moist, plants should thrive and spread by new seedlings each year. Japanese primroses also demand shade (with no more than one hour of direct morning sun). High shade from tall hardwoods or pines works well. While individual plants live only a few years, you will never miss them because new seedlings take their place.

To establish a new planting, set out transplants in the spring or start plants from seed. The time to sow outside is when the seeds ripen—late summer to early fall. Simply scatter the seed over bare soil where you want seedlings to sprout.

Japanese primroses thrive in moist, acid soil and light shade, lending sensational color to the banks of a pond when planted in masses.

Soft shades of Japanese primrose create a light, lacy effect in the spring garden.

Salvia

Anise sage has some of the largest blooms of any salvia. Its azure flowers can be 2 inches long.

Most summer flowers are past their prime in fall. Not so with perennial salvias, which have a way of saving the day. Fall is when many of them come into their full glory, with brilliant spikes of blue, purple, or red flowers.

While many salvias are reliably hardy through Zone 7, a few can be considered perennial only from Zone 8 southward. Yet salvias grow so fast and provide so much color for so little effort that you will want to grow them even if they are only annual in your garden.

You have probably used the popular annual salvia (*Salvia splendens,* or scarlet sage) as a bedding plant for summer color, and you may have grown culinary sage (*Salvia officinalis*) in your herb garden. These are two relatives of perennial flowering salvias and are commonly referred to as sage.

AT A GLANCE
❖
SALVIA
Salvia species

Features: natural, shrublike plants; dramatic color

Colors: blue, purple, red, rose, white

Height: 1 to 6 feet

Light: full sun to partial shade

Soil: average, well drained

Water: medium

Pests: whiteflies

Native: some

Range: Zones 2 to 10

Remarks: easy to grow, blooms for a long time

In the Landscape

Some salvias are shrublike and are therefore impressive as specimens or grouped in borders. Because of this, they make good back-of-the-border plants and may be planted along fences and in herb gardens. For contrast, pair blue and purple salvias with strong yellow flowers, such as coneflowers, sunflowers, mums, or marigolds. Or group several blue and white salvias together for a clean, natural effect; add pink yarrow, lamb's ears, or Shasta daisies for a cottage touch. Perennial salvias can be the primary feature of the landscape during the growing season, adding low-maintenance color for up to six months. Smaller selections add visual impact in containers.

A fall salvia, Mexican bush sage mixes well with yellow swamp sunflowers and the burgundy foliage of Red Shield hibiscus.

Species and Selections

Mexican bush sage or velvet sage *(Salvia leucantha)* is a fall salvia with thin gray-green leaves and abundant fuzzy purple flowers atop 15- to 20-inch spikes. It blooms from late summer to the first frost on plants that grow 3 to 4 feet tall, sometimes taller in warm areas. Emerald is a selection with purple spikes and white centers; All Purple has entirely purple flowers. Mexican bush sage is not perennial north of Zone 8 but reaches its full size even if grown as an annual. A single-stemmed transplant set in the garden in late spring will reward you with a vase-shaped plant that is 4 feet tall and equally wide by the time it blooms in September. Mexican bush sage is an unusually pretty cut flower; hang bouquets upside down in a breezeway to dry them to perfection.

Brazilian sage *(Salvia guaranitica)*, another late bloomer, boasts the largest flowers of all salvias and has foliage with a faint spicy scent. Wisps of 1½- to 2-inch-long bluish purple flowers appear on the 3-foot plants all summer. Some selections reach 5 or 6 feet. It is best used as an annual in all but the Lower and Coastal South, planted in well-drained soil in light shade. A native of South America, this salvia is a favorite of hummingbirds and works well in wildflower and butterfly gardens. Argentina Skies has pale blue flowers.

Autumn sage *(Salvia greggii)* is native to Texas. It is perennial in the Lower and Coastal South, where it blooms generously from spring until frost (despite its name). It puts on an equally impressive show as an annual farther north. Autumn sage boasts dozens of sparkling blooms in magenta, red, coral, or white. Because it is open in form, this salvia should be paired with solid-colored, fuller flowers, such as Queen Anne's lace or white daisies. Autumn sage is drought tolerant and does not mind alkaline soil or heavy soil, even red clay. Give it full or partial shade.

Autumn sage is brilliant in fall with magenta, white, or pale red flowers.

Mealy-cup sage *(Salvia farinacea)* is one of the best known perennial salvias and is the most readily available. It is native to Texas and other parts of the Southwest. Although mealy-cup sage is neither dependably perennial nor long-lived, gardeners who grow it as an annual come to rely on its continuous flowers from early summer until frost. Victoria is one of the hardiest selections, with rich, deep blue flowers. The plants will grow about 1½ feet tall and bloom all summer long. Blue Bedder is less hardy; it has light blue flowers and may reach 2 feet tall. White Porcelain is a selection with white blooms that grows about 15 inches tall. Prune this salvia if it begins to look leggy (usually in August). With extra watering, it comes back with a passion in fall. It also does double duty as a cut flower—fresh or dried.

Pineapple sage offers fragrant foliage topped by the truest red flowers of fall.

Pineapple sage *(Salvia elegans)* hails from Mexico and is appreciated for its delicate red flowers and the fruity fragrance of its leaves, which can be used fresh or dried in cakes, teas, and herbal seasonings. This plant is sometimes labeled *Salvia rutilans*. Like Mexican bush sage, this salvia waits until fall to yield a floral display, but it provides a grand finale to summer. It is not always cold hardy north of Zone 9.

Forsythia salvia *(Salvia madrensis)* is an unusual yellow-flowered species. It is a good companion to fall-blooming perennials, as its blooms do not open until October.

Hybrid salvias are also available for the perennial garden. Indigo Spires has rich purple flowers that stand above leafy green foliage. Plants grow 3 to 6 feet tall; the flower stalks become longer (18 to 20 inches) and deeper in color in fall. This is a good salvia for beginners as it has many uses, performs well, and can be mixed with other blooms. It is one of the hardiest salvias, growing in Zones 3 to 8. East Friesland is another popular hybrid with deep purple blooms; it grows only about 1½ feet tall. May Night is a similar selection but is a bit less tolerant of hot, humid weather.

Planting and Care

Good drainage is a must for growing salvias—they will rot in soggy soil. However, they like plenty of water during summer, especially in August. Many salvias are drought tolerant, but they all need ample water to help fuel rapid growth and high performance. Most need full sun (at least six hours) for best blooming.

Tall plants may require staking, although pinching back outer branches helps support the inner ones. Pairing tall salvias with shorter, shrubbier plants also provides support. Cut back salvias after they freeze and mulch them for protection against winter cold. Prune Mexican bush sage in early summer to keep it compact.

To propagate salvia, divide clumps in spring or fall. For tender perennials, take 4- to 6-inch cuttings, remove the flower stalks, and set them in containers filled with moist sand; overwinter them indoors, beside a basement window or in a greenhouse or cold frame.

Troubleshooting

Pests and disease problems are minimal, although whiteflies can sometimes bother salvia. See page 236 for more about whiteflies.

The flowering stalks of Indigo Spires grow longer and more intensely colored as fall progresses.

Sedum

Showy sedum is a natural companion to arching ornamental grasses.

Showy sedum is one of the most rugged, durable perennials available. This plant is tailor-made for gardeners whose intentions are greater than their time. As long as they get plenty of light, sedums rarely disappoint, blooming in spite of forgotten waterings and a complete lack of plant food.

This late bloomer emerges in spring with succulent rosettes of leaves that grow into lush mounds of gray-green foliage. By mid-summer, flower buds take shape, looking much like beaded tufts atop the pale, smooth foliage that is similar to that of jade plant. In fall, the plants blush with color as the buds open into starlike clusters of pink, rose, crimson, or copper.

In the Landscape

Showy sedum combines nicely with shrubs and other perennials. Plant it with yellow mums, ornamental grasses, coneflowers, or asters. You can also use it to provide textural contrast for finer leafed shrubs, such as Scotch broom and cotoneaster. Mix showy sedum with plants bearing gray-green foliage, such as lamb's ears, fernleaf yarrow, Silver Mound artemisia, or bearded iris. Because it is so drought tolerant, sedum is a choice plant to feature in an urn or other ornamental container. Place it to mark an entrance, to serve as the focal point of a path, or to add a spot of color on your terrace, deck, or patio. Thriving in full sun and clay soil, showy sedum has long been popular in rock gardens. But more gardeners are finding that sedums also make ideal perennials for borders, containers, and beds.

Different Selections

The species has soft pink blooms and is often found in old gardens. Selections display a fascinating range of shades as their flowers bloom and deepen. For example, the selection known as Autumn Joy (also called Indian Chief) blossoms from pale green buds into rich pink flowers, progresses to a salmon shade of bronze, and dries to a coppery red that persists into winter. Brilliant is raspberry red, Meteor has deep red blooms, and Star Dust is ivory with occasional pink flowers.

At a Glance
❖
Showy Sedum
Sedum spectabile

Features: succulent leaves, striking flowers

Colors: pink, red, bronze

Height: 1 to 2 feet

Light: full sun to partial shade

Soil: well drained

Water: low

Pests: none specific

Native: no

Range: Zones 4 to 9

Remarks: easy to grow, long-lived

Its attractive, succulent mound of leaves and sculptural form make sedum an asset even when it is not in bloom.

Planting and Care

Showy sedum enjoys full sun but also grows in light shade; plants in shade may require pruning back in early summer so that they do not get too leggy. The only conditions in which showy sedum will not grow are deep shade and poor drainage.

Set out transplants or divisions in the fall or early spring. Watering is necessary only during severe drought. Do not mulch showy sedum as this promotes rot. To propagate sedum, snip off a stem, plant it in moist soil, and watch it take root.

In the fall Autumn Joy sedum slowly turns from a rich pink to a coppery red, drying on the stem. Here it grows with narrow-leaf zinnia and mealy-cup sage.

Yarrow

Common yarrow brings deep pink to the color palette in the garden.

When yarrow blooms, it is as if the brilliant yellow sun had broken through a mask of sullen clouds. This is why many flower borders feature yarrow in late spring, summer, and occasionally in fall.

But not all yarrows are yellow. Unlike fernleaf yarrow, the yellow type, common yarrow sports flowers of pink and white. Your choice of yarrow depends on where you live and what kind of effect you want to create. Either type is a fine addition to the garden—informal, hardy, and colorful with delicate, fernlike foliage that is attractive even when the plants are not in bloom.

Yarrow is also a choice cut flower, fresh or dried. For drying and preserving, cut the flowers when they are at their peak. Use a rubber band to bind the ends of the stems together, and hang the bunch upside down in a cool, dry, dark place. The flowers will be ready for arranging in three to four weeks.

Common yarrow adapts well to flower borders in hot, humid climates.

In the Landscape

Yarrow has long been a staple of herb gardens. Today it is a pleasant addition to garden borders, meadows, and mass plantings in full sun. For a mix of color and texture, try combining yarrow with pink phlox or purple-leafed plants. Other excellent companions include blue salvia and ornamental grasses.

Species and Selections

Fernleaf yarrow (*Achillea filipendulina*) makes an excellent garden plant because it stands up straight and stays where you put it. It also possesses handsome foliage that ranges from gray-green to silver. The main flush of yellow bloom appears in late May or early June and lasts about a month. Sporadic blooms then appear throughout the summer. The largest selection of fernleaf yarrow is Gold Plate, which grows 4 to 5 feet tall and nearly as wide. Its flattened clusters of tiny golden blossoms may be 6 inches across. This plant is strictly for the

---

AT A GLANCE

❖

YARROW

Achillea species

Features: billowy flower clusters in summer

Colors: yellow, white, deep pink

Height: 1 to 5 feet

Light: full sun

Soil: average, well drained

Water: medium

Pests: none specific

Native: no

Range: Zones 3 to 9

Remarks: needs good air circulation

rear of large perennial borders. Another back-of-the-border yarrow is Parker's Variety. It grows 3 to 4 feet tall with clusters about 3 inches across. Either of these plants may require staking if planted in rich soils or overfertilized.

Common yarrow *(Achillea millefolium)* is a native of Europe that has been naturalized in this country, where it is a prolific spreader. Some consider it a weed, but if divided regularly in the fall and not overfertilized, common yarrow remains compact. It is the best yarrow for hot, humid environments. Ranging from 1 to 2 feet in height, common yarrow is covered in fine, ferny foliage and blooms from late spring to summer, and occasionally again in the fall. It is both heat and drought tolerant, hence excellent for an untended or wild area. Colors include white and rosy pink; Fire King is one of the more popular pinks on the market.

Hybrid yarrows include Coronation Gold, a hybrid between fernleaf yarrow and *Achillea clypeolata* that enjoys popularity in the South. Growing 2½ to 3 feet tall, it is ideal for the middle or rear of a small flower border. Its deep golden clusters, about 3 inches across, appear atop fine, silvery green foliage. Another popular hybrid is Moonshine. This is much lower growing than other yarrows—about 1½ to 2 feet—so use it at the front of a border. Its gray foliage and canary yellow blooms are its highlights; this lighter shade is easy to blend with other flower colors. The only drawback to fernleaf yarrow and some of its hybrids is that they have not proven to be as hardy in the hot, humid Coastal South.

The Pearl *(Achillea ptarmica* The Pearl) is a popular hybrid that bears clusters of white buttonlike flowers. It tends to sprawl and flop, so plant it where it can spill over an edge.

Planting and Care

Planted in the right place, yarrow is easy to grow. These perennials tolerate heat and drought but cannot stand hot, humid weather. They need bright sunshine and excellent drainage and air circulation to help protect the foliage from humid weather. Good drainage is especially important in winter, when yarrow is most susceptible to root rot. Divide every couple of years to rejuvenate and prevent overcrowding. Faithful deadheading will help keep the plant blooming all summer.

The flattened clusters of fernleaf yarrow contain hundreds of tiny blossoms.

Pests and Diseases

The following insects and diseases are common pests of the plants in this book. To control them, you must first know your enemy; learn which plants are susceptible, what symptoms may occur, and how to combat the pests. Many techniques and pesticides are available to help you fight diseases and pests, but the recommendations for these products frequently change. Contact your county Extension Service office for information about specific pesticides.

Before using a pesticide, read the entire label. Always use pesticides strictly according to label directions. Using a pesticide in any way that is not in accordance with label recommendations is illegal.

Aphids

Aphids

Aphids are tiny, pear-shaped insects about ⅛ to ¼ inch long; they are frequently green or black but may also be yellow or pink. They harm plants by sucking sap from the tender young stems and flower buds so that growth is distorted and the buds do not open. Aphids are usually worst in spring and fall. They will produce hundreds of offspring in a few weeks, so it is crucial to control them as soon as they appear.

Cabbageworms and Other Caterpillars

Cabbageworms are green, velvety caterpillars that chew holes in leaves. They are primarily pests of the vegetable garden but will attack ornamental cabbage and kale, which are relatives of the culinary types. Control caterpillars as soon as you can because their feeding will disfigure the leaves. They hide on the underside of the leaves and in the crown of the plant; spray or dust these areas very carefully.

Other caterpillars may attack the leaves and buds of annuals, especially those with large, succulent leaves. To control these pests, spray the underside of the leaves thoroughly and keep caterpillar dust on the foliage to prevent reinfestation.

Hollyhock Rust

This disease can destroy an entire planting of hollyhocks. Signs of the disease are yellow areas on the surface of the leaves and orange, rustlike spots on the underside. You may also see long, dark lesions on the stalks. The best way to control rust is to purchase selections that are rust resistant. Remove old plants from the garden once they have faded; if left untended, they provide a source for infection the following year. For plants that are already infected, spray both sides of the leaves and the stems with a recommended fungicide.

Japanese Beetles

These ½-inch-long, metallic green-and-copper beetles will fly into your garden and are very difficult to control. They feed on many plants but are especially fond of hollyhocks. Japanese beetles like to chew one plant for a short time and then fly to another plant. They usually feed in hordes, with hundreds present at a time.

Dusting foliage with a recommended pesticide helps, but you must keep the dust on new growth as it unfurls. The best way to control Japanese beetles is to kill the **grubs,** or larvae, which feed in the lawn. To do this most effectively, join forces with neighbors, who are doubtless being affected by this pest as well, to treat a large area.

Japanese beetle

Nematodes

Nematodes are soil-borne microscopic creatures that attack the roots of many plants. Their feeding prevents the roots from functioning properly, so plants become stunted and may die. Unfortunately, there is no simple solution to nematodes. Strategies include removing the soil, switching to less susceptible plants, and maintaining the overall health of the plants in your garden. Contact your Extension Service office for more information.

Powdery Mildew

Powdery mildew is a disease that looks like a white to gray mildew on the surface of the leaves. It causes the leaves to dry and wither, thus weakening the plant. To control powdery mildew, be sure that plants are not crowded; good air circulation helps to keep the foliage dry so that powdery mildew will not develop.

Once the disease appears, it is difficult to control. Therefore, you should spray both sides of the leaves with an approved fungicide before the mildew appears. If you have seen the disease in your garden before, you can generally predict its reoccurrence (usually in spring and fall).

Powdery mildew is likely to affect celosia and zinnias. To avoid the problem, look for selections that have been bred with resistance to the disease.

Powdery mildew

Slug

Spider mite damage

Slugs

Slugs are like snails without shells. They chew holes in the succulent leaves of young plants. Slugs feed at night, so you will not see them unless you turn over a rock or a handful of mulch to find where they hide during the day. One sure sign of slugs is a shiny slime trail on the leaves in your garden. To see the trail clearly, hold an affected leaf in the sunlight and turn it so that the light is reflected by the slimy trail.

You can control slugs with bait, but read the label warning carefully, as most are poisonous to pets. You can trap slugs in shallow bowls of beer or beneath cantaloupe or grapefruit halves turned upside down in the garden. If you have a pond or water garden, bring in toads, which will eat slugs.

Spider Mites

Spider mites are tiny spiderlike insects that collect on the underside of the leaves and on flower buds. They damage plants by sucking sap from the plants so that the leaves are deformed and the buds do not open. They are worst in spring and fall, especially during dry weather. You may not see the spider mites until their feeding begins to make the topside of the leaves look faded and mottled. Turning a leaf over will reveal clusters of pinpoint-sized spider mites and often their delicate webbing. Use a magnifying glass to be sure.

To control spider mites, spray the underside of the leaves thoroughly. Spider mites love hollyhock, lantana, rose verbena, and sweet pea, so look for them on these plants in particular.

Whiteflies

These white, mothlike insects are only ⅛ inch long and can usually be seen on the underside of young leaves. If you shake the plant, they will fly out and then light again. They suck sap from the leaves, leaving foliage yellowed and spotted. Ageratum, geranium, lantana, and rose verbena are favorites of this pest. To control whiteflies, spray the underside of the leaves with a recommended pesticide.

Index

Index

Index

Special Thanks

All-America Selections, photograph, 163

Ball Seed Company

Jim Bathie, photographs, 28, 29, 30, 31, 45 (top right)

David Durham, photograph, 82

Jacqueline Giovanelli

Goldsmith Seeds, Inc.

Jennifer Greer

Oak Street Garden Shop

PanAmerican Seed Company

Suzanne Powell

Catherine Ritter Scholl

Southern Progress Corporation Library Staff

White Flower Farm/Michael Dodge, photograph, 166